FOREIGN AFFAIRS

Special Collection

CRITICAL GLOBAL CHALLENGES

The Year of Living Dangerously

Was 2014 a Watershed?

Gideon Rose

In January 2014, "Crimea," "the Caliphate," and "Sykes-Picot" were terms students learned in history courses. People knew Isis as an Egyptian goddess and thought the United States was out of Iraq for good. Nobody expected a global Ebola crisis and everybody expected oil prices to stay high indefinitely.

In January 2015, things look rather different. According to an increasingly common narrative, the liberal international order that emerged at the end of World War II and spread after the end of the Cold War is now in decline. The United States is in retreat; China, Russia, Iran, and other challengers are on the march. War has returned to Europe, the Middle East is in turmoil, and Asia is a tinderbox waiting to explode.

A few scattered optimists beg to differ. They point out that the crises have occurred in the periphery, not the core. The farther reaches of Eastern Europe may be contested, but the rest of the continent remains safe and secure, nestling under an iron-clad nato security guarantee. Iraq and Syria may have collapsed, but the rest of the region has not followed suit, and global energy supplies have never been more plentiful. China may be determined to flex its geopolitical muscles, but the more it does so the more it scares its neighbors and provokes a balancing coalition. And for all its dysfunction, the United States remains the dominant global player,

GIDEON ROSE is Editor of *Foreign Affairs*.

has the developed world's most dynamic economy, and is at the forefront of revolutions in energy, information technology, and other areas.

So much is going on that it is hard to get a handle on it all, let alone to tie things together neatly in a simple framework. But at *Foreign Affairs*, we have been carefully tracking the emergence and debating the significance of this "new global context," as the World Economic Forum puts it, in real time. So we decided that it would be useful to put together this special collection as background reading for the Forum's 2015 Annual Meeting.

Drawn from the pages of our print magazine and the pixels of our website, the articles gathered here trace major recent geopolitical events and debates from a broad range of expert perspectives. They give you the information and argumentation you need to make up your own mind about what truly matters, why, and what might come next.

The first section treats the biggest questions of them all: just how much trouble the liberal international order is in and whether it is likely to advance or retreat in years to come.

The second section explores the crisis in Ukraine, asking why it happened, who was responsible for what, and where things go from here.

The third section moves to Asia, noting Xi Jinping's increasingly tight grip and the complexities of China's relationships with the United States, Russia, and Japan.

The fourth section examines the chaos in the Middle East, asking whether the region's modern state system is really dissolving, who is doing what about the Islamic State, and how much of a threat returning jihadists pose for the West.

The fifth section, finally, tackles some of the trends reshaping the global economy—the shale revolution, the rise of robotics and artifical intelligence, and the future of world trade.

2014 witnessed more breaks from its predecessor than anybody expected, and 2015 could easily follow suit. Yet what's past is prologue, as the poet said, and so a collection such as this should cast light forward as well as backward, illuminating the obstacles and opportunities that lie ahead as well as those behind. If nothing else, it offers a sobering reminder that the old adage is spot on: prediction is hard, especially about the future.

Business in a Changing World

Stewarding the Future

Klaus Schwab   JANUARY 6, 2015

The business of doing business, by which I mean transforming resources into products and services in the most efficient and sustainable way, has never been more challenging, yet at the same time, the opportunities have never been greater. The transformative forces underway—driven by the world's increasing complexity, interconnectivity, and velocity, as well as a rapidly changing geopolitical environment—create a need for new models of engagement among business, government, and civil society to address the shortcomings of our existing multilateral governance system and the critical challenges of our times. By serving as a responsible and responsive stakeholder in the global community, global business has a unique role to play in safeguarding our collective future. The urgent task now is to define how it best fulfills this role and the qualities its leaders must possess to do so effectively.

The concept of corporate social responsibility (CSR) has long been used as an effective lens through which to examine the actions business can take toward ensuring mutual long-term well-being and sustainability. CSR provides context on the role of business in the global community, benchmarking business

KLAUS SCHWAB is Founder and Executive Chairman of the World Economic Forum. A version of this article originally appeared in the book *Business in a Changing Society: Festschrift for Peter Brabeck-Letmathe* (November 2014).

performance against its responsibilities to society and the environment as well as to shareholders. Yet the definition of CSR has become increasingly broad, referring to anything from the health and safety of workers to sustainable sourcing or philanthropy. CSR alone, therefore, is not sufficient to help optimize corporate behavior and decision-making, and should be supplemented with five other pillars of a company's engagement with its stakeholders: corporate governance, corporate philanthropy, corporate social entrepreneurship, global corporate citizenship, and professional accountability.

Corporate governance refers to how a company is run—in accordance with local and international law, transparency and accountability requirements, ethical norms, and environmental codes of conduct. Essentially, it is a corporation's basic "license to operate." Absent good corporate governance, no collaboration with the wider stakeholder universe is possible. A good example of an initiative that successfully binds corporations to a common set of core principles relating to human rights, labor, the environment, and anti-corruption in this way is the United Nations Global Compact. Launched at the World Economic Forum's Annual Meeting in 1999, the Global Compact is now observed on a voluntary basis by 12,000 corporations across 145 countries.

Corporate philanthropy includes contributions by a company to entities or initiatives outside of its core business activities. Such philanthropy can be extended in a number of ways, from direct donations to the provision of practical support on various projects— whether the construction of a public building, relief in the aftermath of a disaster, or any other activity that delivers a social return. A related form of corporate philanthropy is social investing, which involves funding projects or groups that pursue social goals, such as development agencies or affordable housing schemes. Employees can also engage by directing a portion of their salaries to good causes. The important distinction of corporate philanthropy is that the donor's involvement starts and ends with the contribution or investment.

Corporate social entrepreneurship represents a way of creating innovative products or services that deliver social and environmental benefits. Here, revenue generated through the sale of such offerings can be used to achieve greater scale, delivering an even greater benefit and ensuring the delivery over a longer period of time. As in corporate philanthropy, business' involvement in social entrepreneurship can come in the form of direct investment, in-kind support, or a combination of the two.

If corporate philanthropy and corporate social entrepreneurship focus on the micro, then *global corporate citizenship* represents business' engagement in macro global issues, such as food security, climate change, and cybersecurity. In today's globalized world, where the pace and direction of development is increasingly being shaped by forces beyond the control of nation-states, businesses have not only the right to act to solve shared challenges but a civic obligation to do so—as a stakeholder themselves, in partnership with governments and international organizations. Failure for a global corporation to act in this space means jeopardizing the sustainability of the markets on which it relies, and thus should not be considered an option for any responsible, forward-looking enterprise.

Professional accountability, finally, focuses on the individual character and professional virtues of the people within a global corporation. The long-term productivity, prosperity, and intellectual integrity of our economic and social systems are only possible if the individuals within it act with honesty, moral and intellectual integrity, and humility to embrace an honest, responsive, and responsible work ethic. Creating and maintaining this culture, ensuring diversity, gender equality, and fostering inclusiveness, is essential as we look to mediate the direct effects of our fast-changing world.

It is encouraging to see how far and how fast global business has stepped up to play a leading role in striving to improve the state of our world. It was only in 1971 that I published a book entitled *Modern Management for the Machine Building Industry*, which defined the stakeholder concept for the first time. The Davos Declaration followed two years later, in 1973, articulating the principles behind corporations' social and environmental responsibilities. This decla-ration has shaped the work of the Forum ever since, not to mention the actions of many of its members. Business' track record on all six pillars of global corporate engagement is not without its flaws, however. The culture of corporate excess in certain institutions be-fore, during, and after the global economic crisis has helped to en-trench the dim view of the business community held by some sections of society. Meanwhile, active engagement in global issues has fallen off the agenda in some organizations in the aftermath of the economic crisis.

Global business can and must go further in strengthening its role as a global citizen. It can do this by refining and optimizing the role it plays in existing multi-stakeholder collaborations, and by designing creative and innovative new solutions. Stepping up is by no means an easy task, however. The darkest days of the global economic crisis may be behind us, but we have entered uncertain times. Lower average annual global gdp growth will have a signifi-cant impact on the private sector's ability to create jobs and the governments' ability to deliver quality services. Advances in tech-nology also create further uncertainty, both individually and soci-etally. Whether new technology will create more jobs than it displaces is hard to say, yet few believe that the irreversible trends brought on by technology and innovation will leave any one coun-try, industry, or business untouched by disruption.

Perhaps the greatest challenge, accentuated by globalization and technology, is rising inequality. This growing trend is not sustain-able, and left unaddressed, it threatens the very future of capital-ism. Government must lead by promoting a fair and equitable system, one that benefits all groups in society. Business has a criti-cal role to play, too, by investing in the innovation and talent neces-sary to create high-quality jobs and raise living standards.

All the issues mentioned above are interrelated, yet at the same time they require dramatically different solutions. Playing a posi-tive role as an engaged global corporate citizen in addressing just one of them is a daunting task for any business leader, especially one whose day job is to meet the short-term interests of his or her shareholders. I believe the leaders who succeed in achieving such a truly participatory role in shaping the global agenda must possess three key attributes: contextual intelligence, emotional intelligence, and inspired intelligence.

Contextual intelligence enables leaders to develop a greater awareness and see through the short term imperatives and make better informed, more timely decisions on how best to mobilize resources in ways that deliver the greatest long-term, sustainable value. Emotional intelligence is crucial, not only in decision-making but also in understanding and adapting to the specific needs of partners and fellow stakeholders in developing new models and systems for collaboration. Lastly, inspired intelligence relates to a leader's ability to rise above abstractions that can be overwhelming and lead to paralysis. Maintaining clarity of thought when confronted with both global and local issues is absolutely essential for any leader.

I doubt if any global business leader today would argue that it is not in the long-term interest of his or her organization to act responsibly in the global public interest. The global business community serves as a powerful agent of change—as an engine for innovation and job creation, as a trusted steward of resources, as a protector of rights, and as an agent of resilience. Global business must not only preserve but also strengthen this role, as its future success, like all stakeholders' success, depends on it. In an increasingly sophisticated and globalized world, one facing renewed strains given the new geopolitical context that the past year has borne witness to, the cost of not doing so is simply too great to bear.

The Return of Geopolitics

The Revenge of the Revisionist Powers

Walter Russell Mead   FROM OUR MAY/JUNE 2014 ISSUE

So far, the year 2014 has been a tumultuous one, as geopolitical rivalries have stormed back to center stage. Whether it is Russian forces seizing Crimea, China making aggressive claims in its coastal waters, Japan responding with an increasingly assertive strategy of its own, or Iran trying to use its alliances with Syria and Hezbollah to dominate the Middle East, old-fashioned power plays are back in international relations.

The United States and the EU, at least, find such trends disturbing. Both would rather move past geopolitical questions of territory and military power and focus instead on ones of world order and global governance: trade liberalization, nuclear nonproliferation, human rights, the rule of law, climate change, and so on. Indeed, since the end of the Cold War, the most important objective of U.S. and EU foreign policy has been to shift international relations away from zero-sum issues toward win-win ones. To be dragged back into old-school contests such as that in Ukraine doesn't just divert time and energy away from those important questions; it also changes the character of international politics. As the atmosphere turns dark, the task of promoting and maintaining world order grows more daunting.

WALTER RUSSELL MEAD is James Clarke Chace Professor of Foreign Affairs and Humanities at Bard College and Editor-at-Large of *The American Interest*. Follow him on Twitter @wrmead.

But Westerners should never have expected old-fashioned geo-politics to go away. They did so only because they fundamentally misread what the collapse of the Soviet Union meant: the ideological triumph of liberal capitalist democracy over communism, not the obsolescence of hard power. China, Iran, and Russia never bought into the geopolitical settlement that followed the Cold War, and they are making increasingly forceful attempts to over-turn it. That process will not be peaceful, and whether or not the revisionists succeed, their efforts have already shaken the balance of power and changed the dynamics of international politics.

A FALSE SENSE OF SECURITY

When the Cold War ended, many Americans and Europeans seemed to think that the most vexing geopolitical questions had largely been settled. With the exception of a handful of relatively minor problems, such as the woes of the former Yugoslavia and the Israeli-Palestinian dispute, the biggest issues in world politics, they assumed, would no longer concern boundaries, military bases, na-tional self-determination, or spheres of influence.

One can't blame people for hoping. The West's approach to the realities of the post–Cold War world has made a great deal of sense, and it is hard to see how world peace can ever be achieved without replacing geopolitical competition with the construction of a liberal world order. Still, Westerners often forget that this project rests on the particular geopolitical foundations laid in the early 1990s.

In Europe, the post–Cold War settlement involved the unifica-tion of Germany, the dismemberment of the Soviet Union, and the integration of the former Warsaw Pact states and the Baltic repub-lics into NATO and the EU. In the Middle East, it entailed the dominance of Sunni powers that were allied with the United States (Saudi Arabia, its Gulf allies, Egypt, and Turkey) and the double containment of Iran and Iraq. In Asia, it meant the uncontested dominance of the United States, embedded in a series of security relationships with Japan, South Korea, Australia, Indonesia, and other allies.

This settlement reflected the power realities of the day, and it was only as stable as the relationships that held it up. Unfortunately, many observers conflated the temporary geopolitical conditions of the post–Cold War world with the presumably more final outcome of the ideological struggle between liberal democracy and Soviet communism. The political scientist Francis Fukuyama's famous formulation that the end of the Cold War meant "the end of history" was a statement about ideology. But for many people, the collapse of the Soviet Union didn't just mean that humanity's ideological struggle was over for good; they thought geopolitics itself had also come to a permanent end.

At first glance, this conclusion looks like an extrapolation of Fukuyama's argument rather than a distortion of it. After all, the idea of the end of history has rested on the geopolitical consequences of ideological struggles ever since the German philosopher Georg Wilhelm Friedrich Hegel first expressed it at the beginning of the nineteenth century. For Hegel, it was the Battle of Jena, in 1806, that rang the curtain down on the war of ideas. In Hegel's eyes, Napoleon Bonaparte's utter destruction of the Prussian army in that brief campaign represented the triumph of the French Revolution over the best army that prerevolutionary Europe could produce. This spelled an end to history, Hegel argued, because in the future, only states that adopted the principles and techniques of revolutionary France would be able to compete and survive.

Adapted to the post–Cold War world, this argument was taken to mean that in the future, states would have to adopt the principles of liberal capitalism to keep up. Closed, communist societies, such as the Soviet Union, had shown themselves to be too uncreative and unproductive to compete economically and militarily with liberal states. Their political regimes were also shaky, since no social form other than liberal democracy provided enough freedom and dignity for a contemporary society to remain stable.

To fight the West successfully, you would have to become like the West, and if that happened, you would become the kind of wishy-washy, pacifistic milquetoast society that didn't want to fight about anything at all. The only remaining dangers to world peace would come from rogue states such as North Korea, and although such countries might have the will to challenge the West, they would be too crippled by their obsolete political and social structures to rise above the nuisance level (unless they developed nuclear weapons, of course). And thus former communist states, such as Russia, faced a choice. They could jump on the modernization bandwagon and become liberal, open, and pacifistic, or they could cling bitterly to their guns and their culture as the world passed them by.

At first, it all seemed to work. With history over, the focus shifted from geopolitics to development economics and nonproliferation, and the bulk of foreign policy came to center on questions such as climate change and trade. The conflation of the end of geopolitics and the end of history offered an especially enticing prospect to the United States: the idea that the country could start putting less into the international system and taking out more. It could shrink its defense spending, cut the State Department's appropriations, lower its profile in foreign hotspots—and the world would just go on becoming more prosperous and more free.

This vision appealed to both liberals and conservatives in the United States. The administration of President Bill Clinton, for example, cut both the Defense Department's and the State Department's budgets and was barely able to persuade Congress to keep paying U.S. dues to the UN. At the same time, policymakers assumed that the international system would become stronger and wider-reaching while continuing to be conducive to U.S. interests. Republican neo-isolationists, such as former Representative Ron Paul of Texas, argued that given the absence of serious geopolitical challenges, the United States could dramatically cut both military spending and foreign aid while continuing to benefit from the global economic system.

After 9/11, President George W. Bush based his foreign policy on the belief that Middle Eastern terrorists constituted a uniquely dangerous opponent, and he launched what he said would be a long war against them. In some respects, it appeared that the world was back in the realm of history. But the Bush administration's belief that democracy could be implanted quickly in the Arab Middle East, starting with Iraq, testified to a deep conviction that the overall tide of events was running in America's favor.

President Barack Obama built his foreign policy on the conviction that the "war on terror" was overblown, that history really was over, and that, as in the Clinton years, the United States' most important priorities involved promoting the liberal world order, not playing classical geopolitics. The administration articulated an extremely ambitious agenda in support of that order: blocking Iran's drive for nuclear weapons, solving the Israeli-Palestinian conflict, negotiating a global climate change treaty, striking Pacific and Atlantic trade deals, signing arms control treaties with Russia, repairing U.S. relations with the Muslim world, promoting gay rights, restoring trust with European allies, and ending the war in Afghanistan. At the same time, however, Obama planned to cut defense spending dramatically and reduced U.S. engagement in key world theaters, such as Europe and the Middle East.

AN AXIS OF WEEVILS?

All these happy convictions are about to be tested. Twenty-five years after the fall of the Berlin Wall, whether one focuses on the rivalry between the EU and Russia over Ukraine, which led Moscow to seize Crimea; the intensifying competition between China and Japan in East Asia; or the subsuming of sectarian conflict into international rivalries and civil wars in the Middle East, the world is looking less post-historical by the day. In very different ways, with very different objectives, China, Iran, and Russia are all pushing back against the political settlement of the Cold War.

The relationships among those three revisionist powers are complex. In the long run, Russia fears the rise of China. Tehran's worldview has little in common with that of either Beijing or Moscow. Iran and Russia are oil-exporting countries and like the price of oil to be high; China is a net consumer and wants prices low. Political instability in the Middle East can work to Iran's and Russia's advantage but poses large risks for China. One should not speak of a strategic alliance among them, and over time, particularly if they succeed in undermining U.S. influence in Eurasia, the tensions among them are more likely to grow than shrink.

What binds these powers together, however, is their agreement that the status quo must be revised. Russia wants to reassemble as much of the Soviet Union as it can. China has no intention of contenting itself with a secondary role in global affairs, nor will it accept the current degree of U.S. influence in Asia and the territorial status quo there. Iran wishes to replace the current order in the Middle East—led by Saudi Arabia and dominated by Sunni Arab states—with one centered on Tehran.

Leaders in all three countries also agree that U.S. power is the chief obstacle to achieving their revisionist goals. Their hostility toward Washington and its order is both offensive and defensive: not only do they hope that the decline of U.S. power will make it easier to reorder their regions, but they also worry that Washington might try to overthrow them should discord within their countries grow. Yet the revisionists want to avoid direct confrontations with the United States, except in rare circumstances when the odds are strongly in their favor (as in Russia's 2008 invasion of Georgia and its occupation and annexation of Crimea this year). Rather than challenge the status quo head on, they seek to chip away at the norms and relationships that sustain it.

Since Obama has been president, each of these powers has pursued a distinct strategy in light of its own strengths and weaknesses. China, which has the greatest capabilities of the three, has paradoxically been the most frustrated. Its efforts to assert itself in its region have only tightened the links between the United States and its Asian allies and intensified nationalism in Japan. As Beijing's capabilities grow, so will its sense of frustration. China's surge in power will be matched by a surge in Japan's resolve, and tensions in Asia will be more likely to spill over into global economics and politics.

Iran, by many measures the weakest of the three states, has had the most successful record. The combination of the United States' invasion of Iraq and then its premature withdrawal has enabled Tehran to cement deep and enduring ties with significant power centers across the Iraqi border, a development that has changed both the sectarian and the political balance of power in the region. In Syria, Iran, with the help of its longtime ally Hezbollah, has been able to reverse the military tide and prop up the government of Bashar al-Assad in the face of strong opposition from the U.S. government. This triumph of realpolitik has added considerably to Iran's power and prestige. Across the region, the Arab Spring has weakened Sunni regimes, further tilting the balance in Iran's favor. So has the growing split among Sunni governments over what to do about the Muslim Brotherhood and its offshoots and adherents.

Russia, meanwhile, has emerged as the middling revisionist: more powerful than Iran but weaker than China, more successful than China at geopolitics but less successful than Iran. Russia has been moderately effective at driving wedges between Germany and the United States, but Russian President Vladimir Putin's preoccupation with rebuilding the Soviet Union has been hobbled by the sharp limits of his country's economic power. To build a real Eurasian bloc, as Putin dreams of doing, Russia would have to underwrite the bills of the former Soviet republics—something it cannot afford to do.

Nevertheless, Putin, despite his weak hand, has been remarkably successful at frustrating Western projects on former Soviet territory. He has stopped NATO expansion dead in its tracks. He has dismembered Georgia, brought Armenia into his orbit, tightened his hold on Crimea, and, with his Ukrainian adventure, dealt the West an unpleasant and humiliating surprise. From the Western point of view, Putin appears to be condemning his country to an ever-darker future of poverty and marginalization. But Putin doesn't believe that history has ended, and from his perspective, he has solidified his power at home and reminded hostile foreign powers that the Russian bear still has sharp claws.

THE POWERS THAT BE

The revisionist powers have such varied agendas and capabilities that none can provide the kind of systematic and global opposition that the Soviet Union did. As a result, Americans have been slow to realize that these states have undermined the Eurasian geopolitical order in ways that complicate U.S. and European efforts to construct a post-historical, win-win world.

Still, one can see the effects of this revisionist activity in many places. In East Asia, China's increasingly assertive stance has yet to yield much concrete geopolitical progress, but it has fundamentally altered the political dynamic in the region with the fastest-growing economies on earth. Asian politics today revolve around national rivalries, conflicting territorial claims, naval buildups, and similar historical issues. The nationalist revival in Japan, a direct response to China's agenda, has set up a process in which rising nationalism in one country feeds off the same in the other. China and Japan are escalating their rhetoric, increasing their military budgets, starting bilateral crises with greater frequency, and fixating more and more on zero-sum competition.

Although the EU remains in a post-historical moment, the non-EU republics of the former Soviet Union are living in a very different age. In the last few years, hopes of transforming the former Soviet Union into a post-historical region have faded. The Russian occupation of Ukraine is only the latest in a series of steps that have turned eastern Europe into a zone of sharp geopolitical conflict and made stable and effective democratic governance impossible outside the Baltic states and Poland.

In the Middle East, the situation is even more acute. Dreams that the Arab world was approaching a democratic tipping point—dreams that informed U.S. policy under both the Bush and the

Obama administrations—have faded. Rather than building a liberal order in the region, U.S. policymakers are grappling with the unraveling of the state system that dates back to the 1916 Sykes-Picot agreement, which divided up the Middle Eastern provinces of the Ottoman Empire, as governance erodes in Iraq, Lebanon, and Syria. Obama has done his best to separate the geopolitical issue of Iran's surging power across the region from the question of its compliance with the Nuclear Nonproliferation Treaty, but Israeli and Saudi fears about Iran's regional ambitions are making that harder to do. Another obstacle to striking agreements with Iran is Russia, which has used its seat on the UN Security Council and support for Assad to set back U.S. goals in Syria.

Russia sees its influence in the Middle East as an important asset in its competition with the United States. This does not mean that Moscow will reflexively oppose U.S. goals on every occasion, but it does mean that the win-win outcomes that Americans so eagerly seek will sometimes be held hostage to Russian geopolitical interests. In deciding how hard to press Russia over Ukraine, for example, the White House cannot avoid calculating the impact on Russia's stance on the Syrian war or Iran's nuclear program. Russia cannot make itself a richer country or a much larger one, but it has made itself a more important factor in U.S. strategic thinking, and it can use that leverage to extract concessions that matter to it.

If these revisionist powers have gained ground, the status quo powers have been undermined. The deterioration is sharpest in Europe, where the unmitigated disaster of the common currency has divided public opinion and turned the EU's attention in on itself. The EU may have avoided the worst possible consequences of the euro crisis, but both its will and its capacity for effective action beyond its frontiers have been significantly impaired.

The United States has not suffered anything like the economic pain much of Europe has gone through, but with the country facing the foreign policy hangover induced by the Bush-era wars, an increasingly intrusive surveillance state, a slow economic recovery, and an unpopular health-care law, the public mood has soured. On both the left and the right, Americans are questioning the benefits of the current world order and the competence of its architects. Additionally, the public shares the elite consensus that in a post–Cold War world, the United States ought to be able to pay less into the system and get more out. When that doesn't happen, people blame their leaders. In any case, there is little public appetite for large new initiatives at home or abroad, and a cynical public is turning away from a polarized Washington with a mix of boredom and disdain.

Obama came into office planning to cut military spending and reduce the importance of foreign policy in American politics while strengthening the liberal world order. A little more than halfway through his presidency, he finds himself increasingly bogged down in exactly the kinds of geopolitical rivalries he had hoped to transcend. Chinese, Iranian, and Russian revanchism haven't overturned the post–Cold War settlement in Eurasia yet, and may never do so, but they have converted an uncontested status quo into a contested one. U.S. presidents no longer have a free hand as they seek to deepen the liberal system; they are increasingly concerned with shoring up its geopolitical foundations.

THE TWILIGHT OF HISTORY

It was 22 years ago that Fukuyama published The End of History and the Last Man, and it is tempting to see the return of geopolitics as a definitive refutation of his thesis. The reality is more complicated. The end of history, as Fukuyama reminded readers, was Hegel's idea, and even though the revolutionary state had triumphed over the old type of regimes for good, Hegel argued, competition and conflict would continue. He predicted that there would be disturbances in the provinces, even as the heartlands of European civilization moved into a post-historical time. Given that Hegel's provinces included China, India, Japan, and Russia, it should hardly be surprising that more than two centuries later, the disturbances haven't ceased. We are living in the twilight of history rather than at its actual end.

A Hegelian view of the historical process today would hold that substantively little has changed since the beginning of the nineteenth century. To be powerful, states must develop the ideas and institutions that allow them to harness the titanic forces of industrial and informational capitalism. There is no alternative; societies unable or unwilling to embrace this route will end up the subjects of history rather than the makers of it.

But the road to postmodernity remains rocky. In order to increase its power, China, for example, will clearly have to go through a process of economic and political development that will require the country to master the problems that modern Western societies have confronted. There is no assurance, however, that China's path to stable liberal modernity will be any less tumultuous than, say, the one that Germany trod. The twilight of history is not a quiet time.

The second part of Fukuyama's book has received less attention, perhaps because it is less flattering to the West. As Fukuyama investigated what a post-historical society would look like, he made a disturbing discovery. In a world where the great questions have been solved and geopolitics has been subordinated to economics, humanity will look a lot like the nihilistic "last man" described by the philosopher Friedrich Nietzsche: a narcissistic consumer with no greater aspirations beyond the next trip to the mall.

In other words, these people would closely resemble today's European bureaucrats and Washington lobbyists. They are competent enough at managing their affairs among post-historical people, but understanding the motives and countering the strategies of old-fashioned power politicians is hard for them. Unlike their less productive and less stable rivals, post-historical people are unwilling to make sacrifices, focused on the short term, easily distracted, and lacking in courage.

The realities of personal and political life in post-historical societies are very different from those in such countries as China, Iran, and Russia, where the sun of history still shines. It is not just that those different societies bring different personalities and values to the fore; it is also that their institutions work differently and their publics are shaped by different ideas.

Societies filled with Nietzsche's last men (and women) characteristically misunderstand and underestimate their supposedly primitive opponents in supposedly backward societies—a blind spot that could, at least temporarily, offset their countries' other advantages. The tide of history may be flowing inexorably in the direction of liberal capitalist democracy, and the sun of history may indeed be sinking behind the hills. But even as the shadows lengthen and the first of the stars appears, such figures as Putin still stride the world stage. They will not go gentle into that good night, and they will rage, rage against the dying of the light.

The Illusion of Geopolitics

The Enduring Power of the Liberal Order

G. John Ikenberry   FROM OUR MAY/JUNE 2014 ISSUE

W alter Russell Mead paints a disturbing portrait of the United States' geopolitical predicament. As he sees it, an increasingly formidable coalition of illiberal powers—China, Iran, and Russia—is determined to undo the post–Cold War settlement and the U.S.-led global order that stands behind it. Across Eurasia, he argues, these aggrieved states are bent on building spheres of influence to threaten the foundations of U.S. leadership and the global order. So the United States must rethink its optimism, including its post–Cold War belief that rising non-Western states can be persuaded to join the West and play by its rules. For Mead, the time has come to confront the threats from these increasingly dangerous geopolitical foes.

But Mead's alarmism is based on a colossal misreading of modern power realities. It is a misreading of the logic and character of the existing world order, which is more stable and expansive than Mead depicts, leading him to overestimate the ability of the "axis of weevils" to undermine it. And it is a misreading of China and Russia, which are not full-scale revisionist powers but part-time

G. JOHN IKENBERRY is Albert G. Milbank Professor of Politics and International Affairs at Princeton University and George Eastman Visiting Professor at Balliol College, University of Oxford.

spoilers at best, as suspicious of each other as they are of the outside world. True, they look for opportunities to resist the United
States' global leadership, and recently, as in the past, they have
pushed back against it, particularly when confronted in their own
neighborhoods. But even these conflicts are fueled more by
weakness—their leaders' and regimes'—than by strength. They
have no appealing brand. And when it comes to their overriding
interests, Russia and, especially, China are deeply integrated into
the world economy and its governing institutions.

Mead also mischaracterizes the thrust of U.S. foreign policy.
Since the end of the Cold War, he argues, the United States has
ignored geopolitical issues involving territory and spheres of influence and instead adopted a Pollyannaish emphasis on building the
global order. But this is a false dichotomy. The United States does
not focus on issues of global order, such as arms control and trade,
because it assumes that geopolitical conflict is gone forever; it un-
dertakes such efforts precisely because it wants to manage great-
power competition. Order building is not premised on the end of
geopolitics; it is about how to answer the big questions of
geopolitics.

Indeed, the construction of a U.S.-led global order did not begin with the end of the Cold War; it won the Cold War. In the
nearly 70 years since World War II, Washington has undertaken
sustained efforts to build a far-flung system of multilateral institutions, alliances, trade agreements, and political partnerships. This
project has helped draw countries into the United States' orbit. It
has helped strengthen global norms and rules that undercut the
legitimacy of nineteenth-century-style spheres of influence, bids
for regional domination, and territorial grabs. And it has given the
United States the capacities, partnerships, and principles to confront today's great-power spoilers and revisionists, such as they
are. Alliances, partnerships, multilateralism, democracy—these are
the tools of U.S. leadership, and they are winning, not losing, the
twenty-first-century struggles over geopolitics and the world
order.

THE GENTLE GIANT

In 1904, the English geographer Halford Mackinder wrote that the great power that controlled the heartland of Eurasia would command "the World-Island" and thus the world itself. For Mead, Eurasia has returned as the great prize of geopolitics. Across the far reaches of this supercontinent, he argues, China, Iran, and Russia are seeking to establish their spheres of influence and challenge U.S. interests, slowly but relentlessly attempting to dominate Eurasia and thereby threaten the United States and the rest of the world.

This vision misses a deeper reality. In matters of geopolitics (not to mention demographics, politics, and ideas), the United States has a decisive advantage over China, Iran, and Russia. Although the United States will no doubt come down from the peak of hegemony that it occupied during the unipolar era, its power is still unrivaled. Its wealth and technological advantages remain far out of the reach of China and Russia, to say nothing of Iran. Its recovering economy, now bolstered by massive new natural gas resources, allows it to maintain a global military presence and credible security commitments.

Indeed, Washington enjoys a unique ability to win friends and influence states. According to a study led by the political scientist Brett Ashley Leeds, the United States boasts military partnerships with more than 60 countries, whereas Russia counts eight formal allies and China has just one (North Korea). As one British diplomat told me several years ago, "China doesn't seem to do alliances." But the United States does, and they pay a double dividend: not only do alliances provide a global platform for the projection of U.S. power, but they also distribute the burden of providing security. The military capabilities aggregated in this U.S.-led alliance system outweigh anything China or Russia might generate for decades to come.

Then there are the nuclear weapons. These arms, which the United States, China, and Russia all possess (and Iran is seeking), help the United States in two ways. First, thanks to the logic of mutual assured destruction, they radically reduce the likelihood of great-power war. Such upheavals have provided opportunities for past great powers, including the United States in World War II, to entrench their own international orders. The atomic age has robbed China and Russia of this opportunity. Second, nuclear weapons also make China and Russia more secure, giving them assurance that the United States will never invade. That's a good thing, because it reduces the likelihood that they will resort to desperate moves, born of insecurity, that risk war and undermine the liberal order.

Geography reinforces the United States' other advantages. As the only great power not surrounded by other great powers, the country has appeared less threatening to other states and was able to rise dramatically over the course of the last century without triggering a war. After the Cold War, when the United States was the world's sole superpower, other global powers, oceans away, did not even attempt to balance against it. In fact, the United States' geographic position has led other countries to worry more about abandonment than domination. Allies in Europe, Asia, and the Middle East have sought to draw the United States into playing a greater role in their regions. The result is what the historian Geir Lundestad has called an "empire by invitation."

The United States' geographic advantage is on full display in Asia. Most countries there see China as a greater potential danger— due to its proximity, if nothing else—than the United States. Except for the United States, every major power in the world lives in a crowded geopolitical neighborhood where shifts in power routinely provoke counterbalancing—including by one another. China is discovering this dynamic today as surrounding states react to its rise by modernizing their militaries and reinforcing their alliances. Russia has known it for decades, and has faced it most recently in Ukraine, which in recent years has increased its military spending and sought closer ties to the EU.

Geographic isolation has also given the United States reason to champion universal principles that allow it to access various regions of the world. The country has long promoted the open-door policy and the principle of self-determination and opposed colonialism—less out of a sense of idealism than due to the practical realities of keeping Europe, Asia, and the Middle East open for trade and diplomacy. In the late 1930s, the main question facing the United States was how large a geopolitical space, or "grand area," it would need to exist as a great power in a world of empires, regional blocs, and spheres of influence. World War II made the answer clear: the country's prosperity and security depended on access to every region. And in the ensuing decades, with some important and damaging exceptions, such as Vietnam, the United States has embraced postimperial principles.

It was during these postwar years that geopolitics and order building converged. A liberal international framework was the answer that statesmen such as Dean Acheson, George Kennan, and George Marshall offered to the challenge of Soviet expansionism. The system they built strengthened and enriched the United States and its allies, to the detriment of its illiberal opponents. It also stabilized the world economy and established mechanisms for tackling global problems. The end of the Cold War has not changed the logic behind this project.

Fortunately, the liberal principles that Washington has pushed enjoy near-universal appeal, because they have tended to be a good fit with the modernizing forces of economic growth and social advancement. As the historian Charles Maier has put it, the United States surfed the wave of twentieth-century modernization. But some have argued that this congruence between the American project and the forces of modernity has weakened in recent years. The 2008 financial crisis, the thinking goes, marked a world-historical turning point, at which the United States lost its vanguard role in facilitating economic advancement.

Yet even if that were true, it hardly follows that China and Russia have replaced the United States as the standard-bearers of the global economy. Even Mead does not argue that China, Iran, or Russia offers the world a new model of modernity. If these illiberal powers really do threaten Washington and the rest of the liberal capitalist world, then they will need to find and ride the next great wave of modernization. They are unlikely to do that.

THE RISE OF DEMOCRACY

Mead's vision of a contest over Eurasia between the United States and China, Iran, and Russia misses the more profound power transition under way: the increasing ascendancy of liberal capitalist democracy. To be sure, many liberal democracies are struggling at the moment with slow economic growth, social inequality, and political instability. But the spread of liberal democracy throughout the world, beginning in the late 1970s and accelerating after the Cold War, has dramatically strengthened the United States' position and tightened the geopolitical circle around China and Russia.

It's easy to forget how rare liberal democracy once was. Until the twentieth century, it was confined to the West and parts of Latin America. After World War II, however, it began to reach beyond those realms, as newly independent states established self-rule. During the 1950s, 1960s, and early 1970s, military coups and new dictators put the brakes on democratic transitions. But in the late 1970s, what the political scientist Samuel Huntington termed "the third wave" of democratization washed over southern Europe, Latin America, and East Asia. Then the Cold War ended, and a cohort of former communist states in eastern Europe were brought into the democratic fold. By the late 1990s, 60 percent of all countries had become democracies.

Although some backsliding has occurred, the more significant trend has been the emergence of a group of democratic middle powers, including Australia, Brazil, India, Indonesia, Mexico, South Korea, and Turkey. These rising democracies are acting as stakeholders in the international system: pushing for multilateral cooperation, seeking greater rights and responsibilities, and exercising influence through peaceful means.

Such countries lend the liberal world order new geopolitical heft. As the political scientist Larry Diamond has noted, if Argentina, Brazil, India, Indonesia, South Africa, and Turkey regain their economic footing and strengthen their democratic rule, the G-20, which also includes the United States and European countries, "will have become a strong 'club of democracies,' with only Russia, China, and Saudi Arabia holding out." The rise of a global middle class of democratic states has turned China and Russia into outliers—not, as Mead fears, legitimate contestants for global leadership.

In fact, the democratic upsurge has been deeply problematic for both countries. In eastern Europe, former Soviet states and satellites have gone democratic and joined the West. As worrisome as Russian President Vladimir Putin's moves in Crimea have been, they reflect Russia's geopolitical vulnerability, not its strength. Over the last two decades, the West has crept closer to Russia's borders. In 1999, the Czech Republic, Hungary, and Poland entered NATO. They were joined in 2004 by seven more former members of the Soviet bloc, and in 2009, by Albania and Croatia. In the meantime, six former Soviet republics have headed down the path to membership by joining NATO's Partnership for Peace program. Mead makes much of Putin's achievements in Georgia, Armenia, and Crimea. Yet even though Putin is winning some small battles, he is losing the war. Russia is not on the rise; to the contrary, it is experiencing one of the greatest geopolitical contractions of any major power in the modern era.

Democracy is encircling China, too. In the mid-1980s, India and Japan were the only Asian democracies, but since then, Indonesia, Mongolia, the Philippines, South Korea, Taiwan, and Thailand have joined the club. Myanmar (also called Burma) has made cautious steps toward multiparty rule—steps that have come, as China has not failed to notice, in conjunction with warming relations with the United States. China now lives in a decidedly democratic neighborhood.

These political transformations have put China and Russia on the defensive. Consider the recent developments in Ukraine. The economic and political currents in most of the country are inexorably flowing westward, a trend that terrifies Putin. His only recourse has been to strong-arm Ukraine into resisting the EU and remaining in Russia's orbit. Although he may be able to keep Crimea under Russian control, his grip on the rest of the country is slipping. As the EU diplomat Robert Cooper has noted, Putin can try to delay the moment when Ukraine "affiliates with the EU, but he can't stop it." Indeed, Putin might not even be able to accomplish that, since his provocative moves may serve only to speed Ukraine's move toward Europe.

China faces a similar predicament in Taiwan. Chinese leaders sincerely believe that Taiwan is part of China, but the Taiwanese do not. The democratic transition on the island has made its inhabitants' claims to nationhood more deeply felt and legitimate. A 2011 survey found that if the Taiwanese could be assured that China would not attack Taiwan, 80 percent of them would support declaring independence. Like Russia, China wants geopolitical control over its neighborhood. But the spread of democracy to all corners of Asia has made old-fashioned domination the only way to achieve that, and that option is costly and self-defeating.

While the rise of democratic states makes life more difficult for China and Russia, it makes the world safer for the United States. Those two powers may count as U.S. rivals, but the rivalry takes place on a very uneven playing field: the United States has the most friends, and the most capable ones, too. Washington and its allies account for 75 percent of global military spending. Democratization has put China and Russia in a geopolitical box.

Iran is not surrounded by democracies, but it is threatened by a restive pro-democracy movement at home. More important, Iran is the weakest member of Mead's axis, with a much smaller economy and military than the United States and the other great powers. It is also the target of the strongest international sanctions regime ever assembled, with help from China and Russia. The

Obama administration's diplomacy with Iran may or may not succeed, but it is not clear what Mead would do differently to prevent the country from acquiring nuclear weapons. U.S. President Barack Obama's approach has the virtue of offering Tehran a path by which it can move from being a hostile regional power to becoming a more constructive, nonnuclear member of the international community—a potential geopolitical game changer that Mead fails to appreciate.

REVISIONISM REVISITED

Not only does Mead underestimate the strength of the United States and the order it built; he also overstates the degree to which China and Russia are seeking to resist both. (Apart from its nuclear ambitions, Iran looks like a state engaged more in futile protest than actual resistance, so it shouldn't be considered anything close to a revisionist power.) Without a doubt, China and Russia desire greater regional influence. China has made aggressive claims over maritime rights and nearby contested islands, and it has embarked on an arms buildup. Putin has visions of reclaiming Russia's dominance in its "near abroad." Both great powers bristle at U.S. leadership and resist it when they can.

But China and Russia are not true revisionists. As former Israeli Foreign Minister Shlomo Ben-Ami has said, Putin's foreign policy is "more a reflection of his resentment of Russia's geopolitical marginalization than a battle cry from a rising empire." China, of course, is an actual rising power, and this does invite dangerous competition with U.S. allies in Asia. But China is not currently trying to break those alliances or overthrow the wider system of regional security governance embodied in the Association of Southeast Asian Nations and the East Asia Summit. And even if China harbors ambitions of eventually doing so, U.S. security partnerships in the region are, if anything, getting stronger, not weaker. At most, China and Russia are spoilers. They do not have the interests—let alone the ideas, capacities, or allies—to lead them to upend existing global rules and institutions.

In fact, although they resent that the United States stands at the top of the current geopolitical system, they embrace the underlying logic of that framework, and with good reason. Openness gives them access to trade, investment, and technology from other societies. Rules give them tools to protect their sovereignty and interests. Despite controversies over the new idea of "the responsibility to protect" (which has been applied only selectively), the current world order enshrines the age-old norms of state sovereignty and nonintervention. Those Westphalian principles remain the bedrock of world politics—and China and Russia have tied their national interests to them (despite Putin's disturbing irredentism).

It should come as no surprise, then, that China and Russia have become deeply integrated into the existing international order. They are both permanent members of the UN Security Council, with veto rights, and they both participate actively in the World Trade Organization, the International Monetary Fund, the World Bank, and the G-20. They are geopolitical insiders, sitting at all the high tables of global governance.

China, despite its rapid ascent, has no ambitious global agenda; it remains fixated inward, on preserving party rule. Some Chinese intellectuals and political figures, such as Yan Xuetong and Zhu Chenghu, do have a wish list of revisionist goals. They see the Western system as a threat and are waiting for the day when China can reorganize the international order. But these voices do not reach very far into the political elite. Indeed, Chinese leaders have moved away from their earlier calls for sweeping change. In 2007, at its Central Committee meeting, the Chinese Communist Party replaced previous proposals for a "new international economic order" with calls for more modest reforms centering on fairness and justice. The Chinese scholar Wang Jisi has argued that this move is "subtle but important," shifting China's orientation toward that of a global reformer. China now wants a larger role in the International Monetary Fund and the World Bank, greater voice in such forums as the G-20, and wider global use of its currency. That is not the agenda of a country trying to revise the economic order.

China and Russia are also members in good standing of the nuclear club. The centerpiece of the Cold War settlement between the United States and the Soviet Union (and then Russia) was a shared effort to limit atomic weapons. Although U.S.-Russian relations have since soured, the nuclear component of their arrangement has held. In 2010, Moscow and Washington signed the New START treaty, which requires mutual reductions in long-range nuclear weapons.

Before the 1990s, China was a nuclear outsider. Although it had a modest arsenal, it saw itself as a voice of the nonnuclear developing world and criticized arms control agreements and test bans. But in a remarkable shift, China has since come to support the array of nuclear accords, including the Nuclear Nonproliferation Treaty and the Comprehensive Nuclear Test Ban Treaty. It has affirmed a "no first use" doctrine, kept its arsenal small, and taken its entire nuclear force off alert. China has also played an active role in the Nuclear Security Summit, an initiative proposed by Obama in 2009, and it has joined the "P5 process," a collaborate effort to safeguard nuclear weapons.

Across a wide range of issues, China and Russia are acting more like established great powers than revisionist ones. They often choose to shun multilateralism, but so, too, on occasion do the United States and other powerful democracies. (Beijing has ratified the UN Convention on the Law of the Sea; Washington has not.) And China and Russia are using global rules and institutions to advance their own interests. Their struggles with the United States revolve around gaining voice within the existing order and manipulating it to suit their needs. They wish to enhance their positions within the system, but they are not trying to replace it.

HERE TO STAY

Ultimately, even if China and Russia do attempt to contest the basic terms of the current global order, the adventure will be daunting and self-defeating. These powers aren't just up against the United States; they would also have to contend with the most globally organized and deeply entrenched order the world has ever seen, one that is dominated by states that are liberal, capitalist, and democratic. This order is backed by a U.S.-led network of alliances, institutions, geopolitical bargains, client states, and democratic partnerships. It has proved dynamic and expansive, easily integrating rising states, beginning with Japan and Germany after World War II. It has shown a capacity for shared leadership, as exemplified by such forums as the G-8 and the G-20. It has allowed rising non-Western countries to trade and grow, sharing the dividends of modernization. It has accommodated a surprisingly wide variety of political and economic models—social democratic (western Europe), neoliberal (the United Kingdom and the United States), and state capitalist (East Asia). The prosperity of nearly every country—and the stability of its government—fundamentally depends on this order.

In the age of liberal order, revisionist struggles are a fool's errand. Indeed, China and Russia know this. They do not have grand visions of an alternative order. For them, international relations are mainly about the search for commerce and resources, the protection of their sovereignty, and, where possible, regional domination. They have shown no interest in building their own orders or even taking full responsibility for the current one and have offered no alternative visions of global economic or political progress. That's a critical shortcoming, since international orders rise and fall not simply with the power of the leading state; their success also hinges on whether they are seen as legitimate and whether their actual operation solves problems that both weak and powerful states care about. In the struggle for world order, China and Russia (and certainly Iran) are simply not in the game.

Under these circumstances, the United States should not give up its efforts to strengthen the liberal order. The world that Washington inhabits today is one it should welcome. And the grand strategy it should pursue is the one it has followed for decades: deep global engagement. It is a strategy in which the United States ties itself to the regions of the world through trade, alliances, multilateral institutions, and diplomacy. It is a strategy in which the United States establishes leadership not simply through the exercise of power but also through sustained efforts at global problem solving and rule making. It created a world that is friendly to American interests, and it is made friendly because, as President John F. Kennedy once said, it is a world "where the weak are safe and the strong are just."

The Unraveling

How to Respond to a Disordered World

Richard N. Haass

FROM OUR NOVEMBER/
DECEMBER 2014 ISSUE

I n his classic *The Anarchical Society*, the scholar Hedley Bull argued that there was a perennial tension in the world between forces of order and forces of disorder, with the details of the balance between them defining each era's particular character. Sources of order include actors committed to existing international rules and arrangements and to a process for modifying them; sources of disorder include actors who reject those rules and arrangements in principle and feel free to ignore or undermine them. The balance can also be affected by global trends, to varying degrees beyond the control of governments, that create the context for actors' choices. These days, the balance between order and disorder is shifting toward the latter. Some of the reasons are structural, but some are the result of bad choices made by important players—and at least some of those can and should be corrected.

The chief cauldron of contemporary disorder is the Middle East. For all the comparisons that have been made to World War I or the Cold War, what is taking place in the region today most resembles the Thirty Years' War, three decades of conflict that ravaged much of Europe in the first half of the seventeenth century. As with Europe back then, in coming years, the Middle East is

RICHARD N. HAASS is President of the Council on Foreign Relations. Follow him on Twitter @RichardHaass.

likely to be filled with mostly weak states unable to police large swaths of their territories, militias and terrorist groups acting with increasing sway, and both civil war and interstate strife. Sectarian and communal identities will be more powerful than national ones. Fueled by vast supplies of natural resources, powerful local actors will continue to meddle in neighboring countries' internal affairs, and major outside actors will remain unable or unwilling to stabilize the region.

There is also renewed instability on the periphery of Europe. Under President Vladimir Putin, Russia appears to have given up on the proposition of significant integration into the current European and global orders and chosen instead to fashion an alternative future based on special ties with immediate neighbors and clients. The crisis in Ukraine may be the most pronounced, but not the last, manifestation of what could well be a project of Russian or, rather, Soviet restoration.

In Asia, the problem is less current instability than the growing potential for it. There, most states are neither weak nor crumbling, but strong and getting stronger. The mix of several countries with robust identities, dynamic economies, rising military budgets, bitter historical memories, and unresolved territorial disputes yields a recipe for classic geopolitical maneuvering and possibly armed conflict. Adding to the challenges in this stretch of the world are a brittle North Korea and a turbulent Pakistan, both with nuclear weapons (and one with some of the world's most dangerous terrorists). Either could be the source of a local or global crisis, resulting from reckless action or state collapse.

Some contemporary challenges to order are global, a reflection of dangerous aspects of globalization that include cross-border flows of terrorists, viruses (both physical and virtual), and greenhouse gas emissions. With few institutional mechanisms available for stanching or managing them, such flows hold the potential to disrupt and degrade the quality of the system as a whole. And the rise of populism amid economic stagnation and increasing inequality makes improving global governance even more challenging.

The principles informing international order are also in contention. Some consensus exists about the unacceptability of acquiring territory by force, and it was such agreement that undergirded the broad coalition supporting the reversal of Saddam Hussein's attempt to absorb Kuwait into Iraq in 1990. But the consensus had frayed enough over the succeeding generation to allow Russia to escape similar universal condemnation after its taking of Crimea last spring, and it is anyone's guess how much of the world would respond to an attempt by China to muscle in on contested airspace, seas, or territory. International agreement on sovereignty breaks down even more when it comes to the question of the right of outsiders to intervene when a government attacks its own citizens or otherwise fails to meet its sovereign obligations. A decade after UN approval, the concept of "the responsibility to protect" no longer enjoys broad support, and there is no shared agreement on what constitutes legitimate involvement in the affairs of other countries.

To be sure, there are forces of order at work as well. There has been no great-power war for many decades, and there is no significant prospect of one in the near future. China and the United States cooperate on some occasions and compete on others, but even in the latter case, the competition is bounded. Interdependence is real, and both countries have a great deal invested (literally and figuratively) in the other, making any major and prolonged rupture in the relationship a worrisome possibility for both.

Russia, too, is constrained by interdependence, although less so than China given its energy-concentrated economy and more modest levels of external trade and investment. That means sanctions have a chance of influencing its behavior over time. Putin's foreign policy may be revanchist, but Russia's hard- and soft-power resources are both limited. Russia no longer represents anything that appeals to anyone other than ethnic Russians, and as a result, the geopolitical troubles it can cause will remain on Europe's periphery, without touching the continent's core. Indeed, the critical elements of Europe's transformation over the past 70 years—the democratization of Germany, Franco-German reconciliation, economic integration—are so robust that they can reasonably be taken for granted. Europe's parochialism and military weakness may make the region a poor partner for the United States in global affairs, but the continent itself is no longer a security problem, which is a huge advance on the past.

It would also be wrong to look at the Asia-Pacific and assume the worst. The region has been experiencing unprecedented economic growth for decades and has managed it peacefully. Here, too, economic interdependence acts as a brake on conflict. And there is still time for diplomacy and creative policymaking to create institutional shock absorbers that can help reduce the risk of confrontation stemming from surging nationalism and spiraling distrust.

The global economy, meanwhile, has stabilized in the aftermath of the financial crisis, and new regulations have been put in place to reduce the odds and scale of future crises. U.S. and European growth rates are still below historical norms, but what is holding the United States and Europe back is not the residue of the crisis so much as various policies that restrict robust growth.

North America could once again become the world's economic engine, given its stable, prosperous, and open economy; its 470 million people; and its emerging energy self-sufficiency. Latin America is, for the most part, at peace. Mexico is a far more stable and successful country than it was a decade ago, as is Colombia. Questions hovering over the futures of such countries as Brazil, Chile, Cuba, and Venezuela do not alter the fundamental narrative of a region heading in the right direction. And Africa, too, has a growing number of countries in which better governance and economic performance are becoming the norm rather than the exception.

Traditional analytic approaches have little to offer in making sense of these seemingly contradictory trends. One conventional route, for example, would be to frame the international dynamic as one of rising and falling powers, pitting China's advance against the United States' decline. But this exaggerates the United States' weaknesses and underestimates China's. For all its problems, the United States is well positioned to thrive in the twenty-first century, whereas China faces a multitude of challenges, including slowing growth, rampant corruption, an aging population, environmental degradation, and wary neighbors. And no other country is even close to having the necessary mix of capacity and commitment to be a challenger to the United States for global preeminence.

U.S. President Barack Obama was recently quoted as brushing off concerns that things are falling apart, noting that "the world has always been messy" and that what is going on today "is not something that is comparable to the challenges we faced during the Cold War." Such sanguinity is misplaced, however, as today's world is messier, thanks to the emergence of a greater number of meaningful actors and the lack of overlapping interests or mechanisms to constrain the capacity or moderate the behavior of the most radical ones.

Indeed, with U.S. hegemony waning but no successor waiting to pick up the baton, the likeliest future is one in which the current international system gives way to a disorderly one with a larger number of power centers acting with increasing autonomy, paying less heed to U.S. interests and preferences. This will cause new problems even as it makes existing ones more difficult to solve. In short, the post–Cold War order is unraveling, and while not perfect, it will be missed.

THE CAUSES OF THE PROBLEM

Just why have things begun to unravel? For various reasons, some structural, others volitional. In the Middle East, for example, order has been undermined by a tradition of top-heavy, often corrupt, and illegitimate governments; minimal civil society; the curse of abundant energy resources (which often retard economic and political reform); poor educational systems; and various religion-related problems, such as sectarian division, fights between moderates and radicals, and the lack of a clear and widely accepted line between religious and secular spheres. But outside actions have added to the problems, from poorly drawn national borders to recent interventions.

With more than a decade of hindsight, the decision of the United States to oust Saddam and remake Iraq looks even more mistaken than it did at the time. It is not just that the articulated reason for the war—ridding Saddam of weapons of mass destruction—was shown to be faulty. What looms even larger in retrospect is the fact that removing Saddam and empowering Iraq's Shiite majority shifted the country from balancing Iranian strategic ambitions to serving them, in the process exacerbating frictions between Sunni and Shiite Muslims within the country and the region at large.

Nor did regime change have better results in two other countries where it was achieved. In Egypt, the American call for President Hosni Mubarak to leave office contributed to the polarization of the society. Subsequent events demonstrated that Egypt was not yet ready for a democratic transition, and U.S. withdrawal of support from a longtime friend and ally raised questions elsewhere (most notably in other Arab capitals) about the dependability of Washington's commitments. In Libya, meanwhile, the removal of Muammar al-Qaddafi by a combined U.S. and European effort helped create a failed state, one increasingly dominated by militias and terrorists. The uncertain necessity of the intervention itself was compounded by the lack of effective follow-up, and the entire exercise—coming as it did a few years after Qaddafi had been induced to give up his unconventional weapons programs—probably increased the perceived value of nuclear weapons and reduced the likelihood of getting other states to follow Qaddafi's example.

In Syria, the United States expressed support for the ouster of President Bashar al-Assad and then did little to bring it about. Obama went on to make a bad situation worse by articulating a set of redlines involving Syrian use of chemical munitions and then failing to act even when those lines were clearly crossed. This demoralized what opposition there was, forfeited a rare opportunity to weaken the government and change the momentum of the civil war, and helped usher in a context in which the Islamic State of Iraq and al-Sham (ISIS), which has declared itself the Islamic State, could flourish. The gap between rhetoric and action also further contributed to perceptions of American unreliability.

In Asia, too, the chief criticism that can be levied against U.S. policy is one of omission. As structural trends have increased the risks of traditional interstate conflict, Washington has failed to move in a determined fashion to stabilize the situation—not raising the U.S. military's presence in the region significantly in order to reassure allies and ward off challengers, doing little to build domestic support for a regional trade pact, and pursuing insufficiently active or sustained consultations to shape the thinking and actions of local leaders.

With regard to Russia, both internal and external factors have contributed to the deterioration of the situation. Putin himself chose to consolidate his political and economic power and adopt a foreign policy that increasingly characterizes Russia as an opponent of an international order defined and led by the United States. But U.S. and Western policy have not always encouraged more constructive choices on his part. Disregarding Winston Churchill's famous dictum about how to treat a beaten enemy, the West displayed little magnanimity in the aftermath of its victory in the Cold War. NATO enlargement was seen by many Russians as a humiliation, a betrayal, or both. More could have been made of the Partnership for Peace, a program designed to foster better relations between Russia and the alliance. Alternatively, Russia could have been asked to join NATO, an outcome that would have made little military difference, as NATO has become less of an alliance in the classic sense than a standing pool of potential contributors to "coalitions of the willing." Arms control, one of the few domains in which Russia could lay claim to still being a great power, was shunted to the side as unilateralism and minimalist treaties became the norm. Russian policy might have evolved the way it has anyway, even if the United States and the West overall had been more generous and welcoming, but Western policy increased the odds of such an outcome.

As for global governance, international accords are often hard to come by for many reasons. The sheer number of states makes consensus difficult or impossible. So, too, do divergent national interests. As a result, attempts to construct new global arrangements to foster trade and frustrate climate change have foundered. Sometimes countries just disagree on what is to be done and what they are prepared to sacrifice to achieve a goal, or they are reluctant to support an initiative for fear of setting a precedent that could be used against them later. There is thus decidedly less of an "international community" than the frequent use of the phrase would suggest.

Once again, however, in recent years, developments in and actions by the United States have contributed to the problem. The post–Cold War order was premised on U.S. primacy, which was a function of not just U.S. power but also U.S. influence, reflecting a willingness on the part of others to accept the United States' lead. This influence has suffered from what is generally perceived as a series of failures or errors, including lax economic regulation that contributed to the financial crisis, overly aggressive national security policies that trampled international norms, and domestic administrative incompetence and political dysfunction.

Order has unraveled, in short, thanks to a confluence of three trends. Power in the world has diffused across a greater number and range of actors. Respect for the American economic and political model has diminished. And specific U.S. policy choices, especially in the Middle East, have raised doubts about American judgment and the reliability of the United States' threats and promises. The net result is that while the United States' absolute strength remains considerable, American influence has diminished.

WHAT IS TO BE DONE?

Left unattended, the current world turbulence is unlikely to fade away or resolve itself. Bad could become worse all too easily should the United States prove unwilling or unable to make wiser and more constructive choices. Nor is there a single solution to the problem, as the nature of the challenges varies from region to region and issue to issue. In fact, there is no solution of any sort to a situation that can at best be managed, not resolved.

But there are steps that can and should be taken. In the Middle East, the United States could do worse than to adopt the Hippocratic oath and try above all to do no further harm. The gap between U.S. ambitions and U.S. actions needs to be narrowed, and it will normally make more sense to reduce the former than increase the latter. The unfortunate reality is that democratic transformations of other societies are often beyond the means of outsiders to achieve. Not all societies are equally well positioned to become democratic at any given moment. Structural prerequisites may not be in place; an adverse political culture can pose obstacles. Truly liberal democracies may make for better international citizens, but helping countries get to that point is more difficult than often recognized—and the attempts often riskier, as immature or incomplete democracies can be hijacked by demagoguery or nationalism. Promoting order among states—shaping their foreign policies more than their internal politics—is an ambitious enough goal for U.S. policy to pursue.

But if attempts at regime change should be jettisoned, so, too, should calendar-based commitments. U.S. interests in Iraq were not well served by the inability to arrange for the ongoing presence of a residual U.S. force there, one that might have dampened the feuding of Iraqi factions and provided much-needed training for Iraqi security forces. The same holds for Afghanistan, where all U.S. forces are due to exit by the end of 2016. Such decisions should be linked to interests and conditions rather than timelines. Doing too little can be just as costly and risky as doing too much.

Other things outsiders could usefully do in the region include promoting and supporting civil society, helping refugees and displaced people, countering terrorism and militancy, and working to stem the proliferation of weapons of mass destruction (such as by trying to place a meaningful ceiling on the Iranian nuclear program). Degrading ISIS will require regular applications of U.S. airpower against targets inside both Iraq and Syria, along with coordinated efforts with countries such as Saudi Arabia and Turkey to stem the flow of recruits and dollars. There are several potential partners on the ground in Iraq, but fewer in Syria—where action against ISIS must be undertaken in the midst of a civil war. Unfortunately, the struggle against ISIS and similar groups is likely to be difficult, expensive, and long.

In Asia, the prescription is considerably simpler: implement existing policy assiduously. The Obama administration's "pivot," or "rebalance," to Asia was supposed to involve regular high-level diplomatic engagement to address and calm the region's all-too-numerous disputes; an increased U.S. air and naval presence in the region; and the building of domestic and international support for a regional trade pact. All these actions can and should be higher administration priorities, as should a special attempt to explore the conditions under which China might be prepared to reconsider its commitment to a divided Korean Peninsula.

With Russia and Ukraine, what is required is a mixture of efforts designed to shore up Ukraine economically and militarily, strengthen NATO, and sanction Russia. At the same time, Russia should also be offered a diplomatic exit, one that would include assurances that Ukraine would not become a member of NATO anytime soon or enter into exclusive ties with the EU. Reducing European energy dependence on Russia should also be a priority— something that will necessarily take a long time but should be started now. In dealing with Russia and other powers, meanwhile, Washington should generally eschew attempts at linkage, trying to condition cooperation in one area on cooperation in another. Cooperation of any sort anywhere is too difficult to achieve these days to jeopardize it by overreaching.

At the global level, the goal of U.S. policy should still be integration, trying to bring others into arrangements to manage global challenges such as climate change, terrorism, proliferation, trade, public health, and maintaining a secure and open commons. Where these arrangements can be global, so much the better, but where they cannot, they should be regional or selective, involving those actors with significant interests and capacity and that share some degree of policy consensus.

The United States also needs to put its domestic house in order, both to increase Americans' living standards and to generate the resources needed to sustain an active global role. A stagnant and unequal society will be unlikely to trust its government or favor robust efforts abroad. This need not mean gutting defense budgets, however; to the contrary, there is a strong case to be made that U.S. defense spending needs to be increased somewhat. The good news is that the United States can afford both guns and butter, so long as resources are allocated appropriately and efficiently. Another reason to get things right at home is to reduce American vulnerability. U.S. energy security has improved dramatically in recent years, thanks to the oil and gas revolutions, but the same cannot be said about other problems, such as the country's aging public infrastructure, its inadequate immigration policy, and its long-term public finances.

As has recently been noted in these pages, American political dysfunction is increasing rather than decreasing, thanks to weakened parties, powerful interest groups, political finance rules, and demographic changes. Those who suggest that the country is only a budget deal away from comity are as mistaken as those who suggest that the country is only one crisis away from restored national unity. The world can see this, and see as well that a majority of the American public has grown skeptical of global involvement, let alone leadership. Such an attitude should hardly be surprising given the persistence of economic difficulties and the poor track record of recent U.S. interventions abroad. But it is up to the president to persuade a war-weary American society that the world still matters—for better and for worse—and that an active foreign policy can and should be pursued without undermining domestic well-being.

In fact, sensible foreign and domestic policies are mutually reinforcing: a stable world is good for the home front, and a successful home front provides the resources needed for American global leadership. Selling this case will be difficult, but one way to make it easier is to advance a foreign policy that tries to reorder the world rather than remake it. But even if this is done, it will not be enough to prevent the further erosion of order, which results as much from a wider distribution of power and a decentralization of decision-making as it does from how the United States is perceived and acts. The question is not whether the world will continue to unravel but how fast and how far.

What the Kremlin Is Thinking

Putin's Vision for Eurasia

Alexander Lukin   FROM OUR JULY/AUGUST 2014 ISSUE

Soon after the Soviet Union's collapse in 1991, Western leaders began to think of Russia as a partner. Although Washington and its friends in Europe never considered Moscow a true ally, they assumed that Russia shared their basic domestic and foreign policy goals and would gradually come to embrace Western-style democracy at home and liberal norms abroad. That road would be bumpy, of course. But Washington and Brussels attributed Moscow's distinctive politics to Russia's national peculiarities and lack of experience with democracy. And they blamed the disagreements that arose over the former Yugoslavia, Iraq, and Iran on the short time Russia had spent under Western influence. This line of reasoning characterized what could be termed the West's post-Soviet consensus view of Russia.

The ongoing crisis in Ukraine has finally put an end to this fantasy. In annexing Crimea, Moscow decisively rejected the West's rules and in the process shattered many flawed Western assumptions about its motivations. Now U.S. and European officials need a new paradigm for how to think about Russian foreign policy—and if they want to resolve the Ukraine crisis and prevent similar

ALEXANDER LUKIN is Vice President of the Diplomatic Academy of the Russian Ministry of Foreign Affairs and Director of the Center for East Asian and Shanghai Cooperation Organization Studies at the Moscow State Institute of International Relations.

ones from occurring in the future, they need to get better at putting themselves in Moscow's shoes.

BACK TO THE BEGINNING

From Russia's perspective, the seeds of the Ukraine crisis were planted in the Cold War's immediate aftermath. After the Soviet Union collapsed, the West essentially had two options: either make a serious attempt to assimilate Russia into the Western system or wrest away piece after piece of its former sphere of influence. Advocates of the first approach, including the U.S. diplomat George Kennan and Russian liberals, warned that an anti-Russian course would only provoke hostility from Moscow while accomplishing little, winning over a few small states that would end up siding with the West anyway.

But such admonitions went unheeded, and U.S. Presidents Bill Clinton and George W. Bush chose the second path. Forgetting the promises made by Western leaders to Mikhail Gorbachev after the unification of Germany—most notably that they would not expand NATO eastward—the United States and its allies set out to achieve what Soviet resistance had prevented during the Cold War. They trumpeted NATO's expansion, adding 12 new members, including former parts of the Soviet Union, while trying to convince Russia that the foreign forces newly stationed near its borders, in Estonia, Latvia, Lithuania, Poland, and Romania, would not threaten its security. The EU, meanwhile, expanded as well, adding 16 new members of its own during the same period.

Russian leaders were caught off-guard; they had expected that both sides would increase cooperation, remain responsive to each other's interests, and make mutually acceptable compromises. The Russians felt that they had done their part: although never entirely abandoning the idea of national interests, Russia had shown that it was willing to make sacrifices in order to join the prevailing Western-led order. Yet despite an abundance of encouraging words, the West never reciprocated. Instead, Western leaders maintained the zero-sum mindset left over from the Cold War, which they thought they'd won.

It remains hard to say whether a different approach to the post-Soviet states would have produced a better result for the West. What is obvious is that the course Clinton and Bush took empowered those Russians who wanted Moscow to reject the Western system and instead become an independent, competing center of power in the new multipolar world.

Today, the West's continued advance is tearing apart the countries on Russia's borders. It has already led to territorial splits in Moldova and Georgia, and Ukraine is now splintering before our very eyes. Divisive cultural boundaries cut through the hearts of these countries, such that their leaders can maintain unity only by accommodating the interests of both those citizens attracted to Europe and those wanting to maintain their traditional ties to Russia. The West's lopsided support for pro-Western nationalists in the former Soviet republics has encouraged these states to oppress their Russian-speaking populations—a problem to which Russia could not remain indifferent. Even now, more than two decades after the collapse of the Soviet Union, more than six percent of the population in Estonia and more than 12 percent of the population in Latvia, most of them ethnic Russians, do not have the full rights and privileges of citizenship. They cannot vote in national elections, enroll in Russian schools, or, for the most part, access Russian media. The EU, despite its emphasis on human rights outside its borders, has turned a blind eye to this clear violation of basic rights within them. So when it came to Ukraine and the threat of NATO forces appearing in Crimea—a region for which Russia has special feelings and where most residents consider themselves Russian—Moscow decided that there was nowhere left for such minorities to retreat. Russia annexed Crimea in response to the aspirations of a majority of its residents and to NATO's obvious attempt to push Russia's navy out of the Black Sea.

Western leaders were taken aback by Moscow's swift reaction. In late March, General Philip Breedlove, NATO's supreme allied commander for Europe, said with surprise that Russia was acting "much more like an adversary than a partner." But given that NATO has acted that way since its founding—and never changed its approach after the Cold War—Moscow's actions should have been expected. It was only a matter of time before Russia finally reacted to Western encirclement.

In this context, the government of Vladimir Putin has interpreted Western protests about the situation in Ukraine as nothing more than a case of extreme hypocrisy. Indeed, it is difficult to imagine how the Kremlin could think otherwise. Consider the EU's recent criticism of right-wing groups in Ukraine. In March, the EU's foreign policy chief, Catherine Ashton, condemned Right Sector, a militant nationalist group, for attempting to seize the parliament building in Kiev. But the EU had effectively supported Right Sector when it took to the streets to depose the government of Ukrainian President Viktor Yanukovych only months earlier. None of this is surprising, of course; Western leaders have never had any difficulty justifying the actions of such extremist groups when convenient, as when it assisted Croatians fighting in the self-proclaimed republic of Serbian Krajina in 1995 or nationalists in Kosovo in 1997–98.

Western hypocrisy doesn't end there. Washington has regularly chastised Russia for violating the sanctity of Ukraine's borders. Yet the United States and its allies have no leg to stand on when it comes to the principle of territorial integrity. After all, it was not Russia but the West that, in 2010, supported the ruling by the International Court of Justice that Kosovo's unilateral declaration of independence in 2008 did not violate international law. And Moscow repeatedly warned that the precedents set by Western military interventions in such places as Kosovo, Serbia, Iraq, and Libya would undermine the existing system of international law—including the principle of sovereignty as enshrined in the 1975 Helsinki Accords, in which the West formally acknowledged the national boundaries of the Soviet Union, the former Yugoslavia, and the Warsaw Pact states.

In spite of such Western double standards, Moscow has offered up a number of proposals for resolving the Ukraine crisis: the creation of a coalition government that takes into account the interests of the eastern and southern regions, the federalization of the country, the granting of official status to the Russian language, and so on. But Western ideologues seem unlikely to ever accept such proposals. Working with Russia, instead of against it, would mean admitting that someone outside the West is capable of determining what is good and what is bad for other societies.

COLLISION COURSE

Given the growing distance between Russia and the United States and Europe, it was only a matter of time before their two approaches collided in Ukraine, a border state that has long vacillated between the pull of the East and that of the West. The struggle initially played out between opposing Ukrainian political factions: one that advocated signing an association agreement with the EU and another that favored joining the customs union formed by Belarus, Kazakhstan, and Russia.

Western leaders have consistently viewed such Russian-led efforts at regional integration as hostile moves aimed at resurrecting the Soviet Union and creating an alternative to the Western system. Most officials in the United States and Europe thought that bringing Ukraine into alignment with the EU would deliver a heavy blow to those plans, which explains why they interpreted Yanukovych's decision to temporarily postpone the signing of the EU agreement as a Russian victory that called for a counterattack.

Yet Western leaders are woefully misinformed about the idea of Eurasian integration. Neither Russia nor any of the states seeking to join a Eurasian system wants to restore the Soviet Union or openly confront the West. They do, however, believe that in a multipolar world, free nations have a right to create independent associations among themselves. In fact, the ruling elites of many former Soviet republics have long favored the idea of maintaining or re-creating some form of association among their states. In 1991, for example, they created the Commonwealth of Independent States. And of the 15 former Soviet republics, only a few of them, primarily the Baltic states, have used the collapse of the Soviet Union as an opportunity to permanently abandon all ties to the former union and join Western economic and political unions instead. The remaining countries struggled to arrive at a consensus on precisely what role the CIS should play.

In some former Soviet republics, leaders have actively sought to create new forms of integration, such as the Eurasian Economic Community, whose members include Belarus, Kazakhstan, Kyrgyzstan, Russia, and Tajikistan (Uzbekistan suspended its membership in 2008). In others, such as Georgia, Turkmenistan, and Ukraine, the ruling elites considered the commonwealth the primary means for obtaining a civilized divorce from Russia and dividing up the ownership rights and authorities that were previously held by a single, unified state. In most of these countries, at least part of the official establishment and a significant segment of the general population wanted to maintain close relations with Russia and the other former Soviet states. In Georgia and Moldova, for instance, various ethnic minorities feared increasingly assertive nationalist majorities and hoped that Russia would help protect their rights. In other states, including Belarus and Ukraine, significant parts of the populations had such close economic, cultural, and even familial bonds with Russia that they could not imagine a sharp break.

Yet economic problems have long stood in the way of real integration. Although Putin came to power convinced that the collapse of the Soviet Union was "the greatest geopolitical catastrophe" of the twentieth century, he waited a decade—until Russia had gained sufficient economic and political strength—to do anything about it. It wasn't until 2010 that Belarus, Kazakhstan, and Russia launched a customs union, the first real step toward meaningful economic cooperation among post-Soviet states. The union created a territory free from duties and other economic restrictions, and its members now apply common tariffs and other common regulatory measures in their trade with outside countries. Negotiations are currently under way to add Armenia, Kyrgyzstan, and Tajikistan to the union.

In addition to providing economic benefits, Eurasian integration has fostered security cooperation. Like NATO, the Collective Security Treaty Organization—which includes Armenia, Belarus, Kazakhstan, Kyrgyzstan, Russia, and Tajikistan—requires signatories to help assist any member that comes under attack. Many Eurasian countries put a special value on the CSTO; their leaders know that despite assurances from many other countries and organizations, in the event of a real threat from religious extremists or terrorists, only Russia and its allies will come to the rescue.

UNDER GOD, INDIVISIBLE

With economic cooperation a success, political elites in the countries of the customs union are now discussing the formation of a Eurasian political union. As Putin wrote in the Russian newspaper Izvestiya in 2011, Moscow wants the new union to partner with, not rival, the EU and other regional organizations, such as the Association of Southeast Asian Nations and the North American Free Trade Agreement. That would help the member states "establish [themselves] within the global economy," Putin wrote, and "play a real role in decision-making, setting the rules and shaping the future." For such a union to be effective, however, it will need to evolve naturally and voluntarily. Moreover, taking post-Soviet integration to a new level raises the question of what deeper values would lie at its foundation. If the countries of Europe united to champion the values of democracy, human rights, and economic cooperation, then a Eurasian union must stand for its own ideals, too.

Some political thinkers have found the ideological foundation for such a union by looking to history. The concept of a Eurasian space or identity first arose among Russian philosophers and historians who immigrated from communist Russia to western Europe in the 1920s. Like Russian Slavophiles before them, advocates of

Eurasianism spoke of the special nature of Russian civilization and its differences from European society. But they gazed in a different direction: whereas earlier Slavophiles emphasized Slavic unity and contrasted European individualism with the collectivism of Russian peasant communities, the Eurasianists linked the Russian people to the Turkic-speaking peoples—or "Turanians"—of the Central Asian steppe. According to the Eurasianists, the Turanian civilization, which supposedly originated in ancient Persia, followed its own unique political and economic model—essentially, authoritarianism. Although they valued private initiative in general, many of the Eurasianists condemned the excessive dominance of market principles over the state in the West and emphasized the positive role of their region's traditional religions: Orthodox Christianity, Islam, and Buddhism. However dubious the Eurasianists' historical claims about the Turanians may be, this theory now enjoys wide popularity not only among a significant part of the Russian political elite but also in Kazakhstan, Kyrgyzstan, and other Central Asian states where the Turanians' descendants live.

Although the old ideas advanced by today's Eurasianists may seem somewhat artificial, the plan to establish a Eurasian union should not be considered so far-fetched. The culture and values of many former Soviet republics really do differ from what prevails in the West. Liberal secularism, with its rejection of the absolute values that traditional religions hold as divinely ordained, may be on the rise in western Europe and the United States, but in these former Soviet republics, all the major religions—Orthodox Christianity, Islam, Judaism, and Buddhism—are experiencing a revival. Despite the significant differences between them, all these religions reject Western permissiveness and moral relativism, and not for some pragmatic reason but because they find such notions sinful—either unsanctioned or expressly prohibited by divine authority.

Most inhabitants of these post-Soviet states also resent that people in the West consider their outlook backward and reactionary. Their religious leaders, who are enjoying increasing popularity and influence, concur. After all, one can view progress in different ways. If one believes that the meaning of human existence is to gain more political freedoms and acquire material wealth, then Western society is moving forward. But if one thinks, as a traditional Christian does, that Christ's coming was humanity's most important development, then material wealth looks far less important, for this life is fleeting, and suffering prepares people for eternal life, a process that physical riches hinder. Religious traditionalists see euthanasia, homosexuality, and other practices that the New Testament repeatedly condemns as representing not progress but a regression to pagan times. Viewed through this lens, Western society is more than imperfect; it is the very center of sin.

A great majority of Orthodox Christian believers in Russia, Ukraine, Belarus, and Moldova agree with all of this, as do many people in Central Asia. And these beliefs have propelled to power leaders who support the integration of the former Soviet republics. They have also helped Putin succeed in establishing an independent power center in Eurasia. Western meddling, meanwhile, has only served to further consolidate that power.

MOVING FORWARD

The situation in Ukraine remains tense. It might very well follow the example of Moldova, effectively splitting in two. The United States has perceived Russian calls for dialogue as an attempt to dictate unacceptable conditions. In Russia, the continuing strife has fueled the activity of nationalists and authoritarians. The latter group has become especially active of late and is presenting itself as the only force capable of protecting Russia's interests. An uncontrolled escalation of the confrontation could even lead to outright war. The only solution is for the United States and its allies to change their position from one of confrontation to one of constructive engagement.

After all, a diplomatic solution to the Ukraine crisis is still possible. Even during the Cold War, Moscow and the West managed to reach agreements on the neutral status of Austria and Finland.

Those understandings did not in the least undermine the democratic systems or the general European orientation of those countries, and they even proved beneficial to their economies and international reputations. It is no coincidence that it was Finland, a neutral state with strong ties to both the West and the Soviet Union, that hosted the talks leading to the signing of the Helsinki Accords, which played a major role in easing Cold War tensions. The solution to the current crisis similarly lies in providing international guarantees for both Ukraine's neutral status and the protection of its Russian-speaking population. The alternative would be far, far worse: Ukraine could well break apart, drawing Russia and the West into another prolonged confrontation.

Why the Ukraine Crisis Is the West's Fault

The Liberal Delusions That Provoked Putin

John J. Mearsheimer

FROM OUR SEPTEMBER/ OCTOBER 2014 ISSUE

According to the prevailing wisdom in the West, the Ukraine crisis can be blamed almost entirely on Russian aggression. Russian President Vladimir Putin, the argument goes, annexed Crimea out of a long-standing desire to resuscitate the Soviet empire, and he may eventually go after the rest of Ukraine, as well as other countries in eastern Europe. In this view, the ouster of Ukrainian President Viktor Yanukovych in February 2014 merely provided a pretext for Putin's decision to order Russian forces to seize part of Ukraine.

But this account is wrong: the United States and its European allies share most of the responsibility for the crisis. The taproot of the trouble is NATO enlargement, the central element of a larger strategy to move Ukraine out of Russia's orbit and integrate it into the West. At the same time, the EU's expansion eastward and the West's backing of the pro-democracy movement in Ukraine—beginning with the Orange Revolution in 2004—were critical elements, too. Since the mid-1990s, Russian leaders have adamantly opposed NATO enlargement, and in recent years, they have made it clear that they would not stand by while their strategically

JOHN J. MEARSHEIMER is R. Wendell Harrison Distinguished Service Professor of Political Science at the University of Chicago.

important neighbor turned into a Western bastion. For Putin, the illegal overthrow of Ukraine's democratically elected and pro-Russian president—which he rightly labeled a "coup"—was the final straw. He responded by taking Crimea, a peninsula he feared would host a NATO naval base, and working to destabilize Ukraine until it abandoned its efforts to join the West.

Putin's pushback should have come as no surprise. After all, the West had been moving into Russia's backyard and threatening its core strategic interests, a point Putin made emphatically and repeatedly. Elites in the United States and Europe have been blindsided by events only because they subscribe to a flawed view of international politics. They tend to believe that the logic of realism holds little relevance in the twenty-first century and that Europe can be kept whole and free on the basis of such liberal principles as the rule of law, economic interdependence, and democracy.

But this grand scheme went awry in Ukraine. The crisis there shows that realpolitik remains relevant—and states that ignore it do so at their own peril. U.S. and European leaders blundered in attempting to turn Ukraine into a Western stronghold on Russia's border. Now that the consequences have been laid bare, it would be an even greater mistake to continue this misbegotten policy.

THE WESTERN AFFRONT

As the Cold War came to a close, Soviet leaders preferred that U.S. forces remain in Europe and NATO stay intact, an arrangement they thought would keep a reunified Germany pacified. But they and their Russian successors did not want NATO to grow any larger and assumed that Western diplomats understood their concerns. The Clinton administration evidently thought otherwise, and in the mid-1990s, it began pushing for NATO to expand.

The first round of enlargement took place in 1999 and brought in the Czech Republic, Hungary, and Poland. The second occurred in 2004; it included Bulgaria, Estonia, Latvia, Lithuania, Romania, Slovakia, and Slovenia. Moscow complained bitterly from the start.

During NATO's 1995 bombing campaign against the Bosnian Serbs, for example, Russian President Boris Yeltsin said, "This is the first sign of what could happen when NATO comes right up to the Russian Federation's borders. . . . The flame of war could burst out across the whole of Europe." But the Russians were too weak at the time to derail NATO's eastward movement—which, at any rate, did not look so threatening, since none of the new members shared a border with Russia, save for the tiny Baltic countries.

Then NATO began looking further east. At its April 2008 summit in Bucharest, the alliance considered admitting Georgia and Ukraine. The George W. Bush administration supported doing so, but France and Germany opposed the move for fear that it would unduly antagonize Russia. In the end, NATO's members reached a compromise: the alliance did not begin the formal process leading to membership, but it issued a statement endorsing the aspirations of Georgia and Ukraine and boldly declaring, "These countries will become members of NATO."

Moscow, however, did not see the outcome as much of a compromise. Alexander Grushko, then Russia's deputy foreign minister, said, "Georgia's and Ukraine's membership in the alliance is a huge strategic mistake which would have most serious consequences for pan-European security." Putin maintained that admitting those two countries to NATO would represent a "direct threat" to Russia. One Russian newspaper reported that Putin, while speaking with Bush, "very transparently hinted that if Ukraine was accepted into NATO, it would cease to exist."

Russia's invasion of Georgia in August 2008 should have dispelled any remaining doubts about Putin's determination to prevent Georgia and Ukraine from joining NATO. Georgian President Mikheil Saakashvili, who was deeply committed to bringing his country into NATO, had decided in the summer of 2008 to reincorporate two separatist regions, Abkhazia and South Ossetia. But Putin sought to keep Georgia weak and divided—and out of NATO. After fighting broke out between the Georgian government and South Ossetian separatists, Russian forces took control of Abkhazia and South Ossetia. Moscow had made its point. Yet despite this clear warning, NATO never publicly abandoned its goal of bringing Georgia and Ukraine into the alliance. And NATO expansion continued marching forward, with Albania and Croatia becoming members in 2009.

The EU, too, has been marching eastward. In May 2008, it unveiled its Eastern Partnership initiative, a program to foster prosperity in such countries as Ukraine and integrate them into the EU economy. Not surprisingly, Russian leaders view the plan as hostile to their country's interests. This past February, before Yanukovych was forced from office, Russian Foreign Minister Sergey Lavrov accused the EU of trying to create a "sphere of influence" in eastern Europe. In the eyes of Russian leaders, EU expansion is a stalking horse for NATO expansion.

The West's final tool for peeling Kiev away from Moscow has been its efforts to spread Western values and promote democracy in Ukraine and other post-Soviet states, a plan that often entails funding pro-Western individuals and organizations. Victoria Nuland, the U.S. assistant secretary of state for European and Eurasian affairs, estimated in December 2013 that the United States had invested more than $5 billion since 1991 to help Ukraine achieve "the future it deserves." As part of that effort, the U.S. government has bankrolled the National Endowment for Democracy. The nonprofit foundation has funded more than 60 projects aimed at promoting civil society in Ukraine, and the NED's president, Carl Gershman, has called that country "the biggest prize." After Yanukovych won Ukraine's presidential election in February 2010, the NED decided he was undermining its goals, and so it stepped up its efforts to support the opposition and strengthen the country's democratic institutions.

When Russian leaders look at Western social engineering in Ukraine, they worry that their country might be next. And such fears are hardly groundless. In September 2013, Gershman wrote in *The Washington Post*, "Ukraine's choice to join Europe will accelerate the demise of the ideology of Russian imperialism that Putin represents." He added: "Russians, too, face a choice, and Putin may find himself on the losing end not just in the near abroad but within Russia itself."

CREATING A CRISIS

The West's triple package of policies—NATO enlargement, EU expansion, and democracy promotion—added fuel to a fire waiting to ignite. The spark came in November 2013, when Yanukovych rejected a major economic deal he had been negotiating with the EU and decided to accept a $15 billion Russian counteroffer instead. That decision gave rise to antigovernment demonstrations that escalated over the following three months and that by mid-February had led to the deaths of some one hundred protesters. Western emissaries hurriedly flew to Kiev to resolve the crisis. On February 21, the government and the opposition struck a deal that allowed Yanukovych to stay in power until new elections were held. But it immediately fell apart, and Yanukovych fled to Russia the next day. The new government in Kiev was pro-Western and anti-Russian to the core, and it contained four high-ranking members who could legitimately be labeled neofascists.

Although the full extent of U.S. involvement has not yet come to light, it is clear that Washington backed the coup. Nuland and Republican Senator John McCain participated in antigovernment demonstrations, and Geoffrey Pyatt, the U.S. ambassador to Ukraine, proclaimed after Yanukovych's toppling that it was "a day for the history books." As a leaked telephone recording revealed, Nuland had advocated regime change and wanted the Ukrainian politician Arseniy Yatsenyuk to become prime minister in the new government, which he did. No wonder Russians of all persuasions think the West played a role in Yanukovych's ouster.

For Putin, the time to act against Ukraine and the West had arrived. Shortly after February 22, he ordered Russian forces to take Crimea from Ukraine, and soon after that, he incorporated it into Russia. The task proved relatively easy, thanks to the thousands of Russian troops already stationed at a naval base in the Crimean port of Sevastopol. Crimea also made for an easy target since ethnic Russians compose roughly 60 percent of its population. Most of them wanted out of Ukraine.

Next, Putin put massive pressure on the new government in Kiev to discourage it from siding with the West against Moscow, making it clear that he would wreck Ukraine as a functioning state before he would allow it to become a Western stronghold on Russia's doorstep. Toward that end, he has provided advisers, arms, and diplomatic support to the Russian separatists in eastern Ukraine, who are pushing the country toward civil war. He has massed a large army on the Ukrainian border, threatening to invade if the government cracks down on the rebels. And he has sharply raised the price of the natural gas Russia sells to Ukraine and demanded payment for past exports. Putin is playing hardball.

THE DIAGNOSIS

Putin's actions should be easy to comprehend. A huge expanse of flat land that Napoleonic France, imperial Germany, and Nazi Germany all crossed to strike at Russia itself, Ukraine serves as a buffer state of enormous strategic importance to Russia. No Russian leader would tolerate a military alliance that was Moscow's mortal enemy until recently moving into Ukraine. Nor would any Russian leader stand idly by while the West helped install a government there that was determined to integrate Ukraine into the West.

Washington may not like Moscow's position, but it should understand the logic behind it. This is Geopolitics 101: great powers are always sensitive to potential threats near their home territory. After all, the United States does not tolerate distant great powers deploying military forces anywhere in the Western Hemisphere, much less on its borders. Imagine the outrage in Washington if China built an impressive military alliance and tried to include Canada and Mexico in it. Logic aside, Russian leaders have told their Western counterparts on many occasions that they consider NATO expansion into Georgia and Ukraine unacceptable, along with any effort to turn those countries against Russia—a message that the 2008 Russian-Georgian war also made crystal clear.

Officials from the United States and its European allies contend that they tried hard to assuage Russian fears and that Moscow should understand that NATO has no designs on Russia. In addition to continually denying that its expansion was aimed at containing Russia, the alliance has never permanently deployed military forces in its new member states. In 2002, it even created a body called the NATO-Russia Council in an effort to foster cooperation. To further mollify Russia, the United States announced in 2009 that it would deploy its new missile defense system on warships in European waters, at least initially, rather than on Czech or Polish territory. But none of these measures worked; the Russians remained steadfastly opposed to NATO enlargement, especially into Georgia and Ukraine. And it is the Russians, not the West, who ultimately get to decide what counts as a threat to them.

To understand why the West, especially the United States, failed to understand that its Ukraine policy was laying the groundwork for a major clash with Russia, one must go back to the mid-1990s, when the Clinton administration began advocating NATO expansion. Pundits advanced a variety of arguments for and against enlargement, but there was no consensus on what to do. Most eastern European émigrés in the United States and their relatives, for example, strongly supported expansion, because they wanted NATO to protect such countries as Hungary and Poland. A few realists also favored the policy because they thought Russia still needed to be contained.

But most realists opposed expansion, in the belief that a declining great power with an aging population and a one-dimensional economy did not in fact need to be contained. And they feared that enlargement would only give Moscow an incentive to cause trouble in eastern Europe. The U.S. diplomat George Kennan articulated this perspective in a 1998 interview, shortly after the U.S. Senate approved the first round of NATO expansion. "I think the Russians will gradually react quite adversely and it will affect their policies," he said. "I think it is a tragic mistake. There was no reason for this whatsoever. No one was threatening anyone else."

Most liberals, on the other hand, favored enlargement, including many key members of the Clinton administration. They believed that the end of the Cold War had fundamentally transformed international politics and that a new, postnational order had replaced the realist logic that used to govern Europe. The United States was not only the "indispensable nation," as Secretary of State Madeleine Albright put it; it was also a benign hegemon and thus unlikely to be viewed as a threat in Moscow. The aim, in essence, was to make the entire continent look like western Europe.

And so the United States and its allies sought to promote democracy in the countries of eastern Europe, increase economic interdependence among them, and embed them in international institutions. Having won the debate in the United States, liberals had little difficulty convincing their European allies to support NATO enlargement. After all, given the EU's past achievements, Europeans were even more wedded than Americans to the idea that geopolitics no longer mattered and that an all-inclusive liberal order could maintain peace in Europe.

So thoroughly did liberals come to dominate the discourse about European security during the first decade of this century that even as the alliance adopted an open-door policy of growth, NATO expansion faced little realist opposition. The liberal worldview is now accepted dogma among U.S. officials. In March, for example, President Barack Obama delivered a speech about Ukraine in which he talked repeatedly about "the ideals" that motivate Western policy and how those ideals "have often been threatened by an older, more traditional view of power." Secretary of State John Kerry's response to the Crimea crisis reflected this same perspective: "You just don't in the twenty-first century behave in nineteenth-century fashion by invading another country on completely trumped-up pretext."

In essence, the two sides have been operating with different playbooks: Putin and his compatriots have been thinking and acting according to realist dictates, whereas their Western counterparts have been adhering to liberal ideas about international politics. The result is that the United States and its allies unknowingly provoked a major crisis over Ukraine.

BLAME GAME

In that same 1998 interview, Kennan predicted that NATO expansion would provoke a crisis, after which the proponents of expansion would "say that we always told you that is how the Russians are." As if on cue, most Western officials have portrayed Putin as the real culprit in the Ukraine predicament. In March, according to *The New York Times*, German Chancellor Angela Merkel implied that Putin was irrational, telling Obama that he was "in another world." Although Putin no doubt has autocratic tendencies, no evidence supports the charge that he is mentally unbalanced. On the contrary: he is a first-class strategist who should be feared and respected by anyone challenging him on foreign policy.

Other analysts allege, more plausibly, that Putin regrets the demise of the Soviet Union and is determined to reverse it by expanding Russia's borders. According to this interpretation, Putin, having taken Crimea, is now testing the waters to see if the time is right to conquer Ukraine, or at least its eastern part, and he will eventually behave aggressively toward other countries in Russia's neighborhood. For some in this camp, Putin represents a modern-day Adolf Hitler, and striking any kind of deal with him would repeat the mistake of Munich. Thus, NATO must admit Georgia and Ukraine to contain Russia before it dominates its neighbors and threatens western Europe.

This argument falls apart on close inspection. If Putin were committed to creating a greater Russia, signs of his intentions would almost certainly have arisen before February 22. But there is virtually no evidence that he was bent on taking Crimea, much less any other territory in Ukraine, before that date. Even Western leaders who supported NATO expansion were not doing so out of a fear that Russia was about to use military force. Putin's actions in Crimea took them by complete surprise and appear to have been a spontaneous reaction to Yanukovych's ouster. Right afterward, even Putin said he opposed Crimean secession, before quickly changing his mind.

Besides, even if it wanted to, Russia lacks the capability to easily conquer and annex eastern Ukraine, much less the entire country. Roughly 15 million people—one-third of Ukraine's population— live between the Dnieper River, which bisects the country, and the Russian border. An overwhelming majority of those people want to remain part of Ukraine and would surely resist a Russian occupation. Furthermore, Russia's mediocre army, which shows few signs of turning into a modern Wehrmacht, would have little chance of pacifying all of Ukraine. Moscow is also poorly positioned to pay for a costly occupation; its weak economy would suffer even more in the face of the resulting sanctions.

But even if Russia did boast a powerful military machine and an impressive economy, it would still probably prove unable to successfully occupy Ukraine. One need only consider the Soviet and U.S. experiences in Afghanistan, the U.S. experiences in Vietnam and Iraq, and the Russian experience in Chechnya to be reminded that military occupations usually end badly. Putin surely understands that trying to subdue Ukraine would be like swallowing a porcupine. His response to events there has been defensive, not offensive.

A WAY OUT

Given that most Western leaders continue to deny that Putin's behavior might be motivated by legitimate security concerns, it is unsurprising that they have tried to modify it by doubling down on their existing policies and have punished Russia to deter further aggression. Although Kerry has maintained that "all options are on the table," neither the United States nor its NATO allies are prepared to use force to defend Ukraine. The West is relying instead on economic sanctions to coerce Russia into ending its support for the insurrection in eastern Ukraine. In July, the United States and the EU put in place their third round of limited sanctions, targeting mainly high-level individuals closely tied to the Russian government and some high-profile banks, energy companies, and defense firms. They also threatened to unleash another, tougher round of sanctions, aimed at whole sectors of the Russian economy.

Such measures will have little effect. Harsh sanctions are likely off the table anyway; western European countries, especially Germany, have resisted imposing them for fear that Russia might retaliate and cause serious economic damage within the EU. But even if the United States could convince its allies to enact tough measures, Putin would probably not alter his decision-making. History shows that countries will absorb enormous amounts of punishment in order to protect their core strategic interests. There is no reason to think Russia represents an exception to this rule.

Western leaders have also clung to the provocative policies that precipitated the crisis in the first place. In April, U.S. Vice President Joseph Biden met with Ukrainian legislators and told them, "This is a second opportunity to make good on the original promise made by the Orange Revolution." John Brennan, the director of the CIA, did not help things when, that same month, he visited Kiev on a trip the White House said was aimed at improving security cooperation with the Ukrainian government.

The EU, meanwhile, has continued to push its Eastern Partnership. In March, José Manuel Barroso, the president of the European Commission, summarized EU thinking on Ukraine, saying, "We have a debt, a duty of solidarity with that country, and we will work to have them as close as possible to us." And sure enough, on June 27, the EU and Ukraine signed the economic agreement that Yanukovych had fatefully rejected seven months earlier. Also in June, at a meeting of NATO members' foreign ministers, it was agreed that the alliance would remain open to new members, although the foreign ministers refrained from mentioning Ukraine by name. "No third country has a veto over NATO enlargement," announced Anders Fogh Rasmussen, NATO's secretary-general. The foreign ministers also agreed to support various measures to improve Ukraine's military capabilities in such areas as command and control, logistics, and cyberdefense. Russian leaders have naturally recoiled at these actions; the West's response to the crisis will only make a bad situation worse.

There is a solution to the crisis in Ukraine, however—although it would require the West to think about the country in a fundamentally new way. The United States and its allies should abandon their plan to westernize Ukraine and instead aim to make it a neutral buffer between NATO and Russia, akin to Austria's position during the Cold War. Western leaders should acknowledge that Ukraine matters so much to Putin that they cannot support an anti-Russian regime there. This would not mean that a future Ukrainian government would have to be pro-Russian or anti-NATO. On the contrary, the goal should be a sovereign Ukraine that falls in neither the Russian nor the Western camp.

To achieve this end, the United States and its allies should publicly rule out NATO's expansion into both Georgia and Ukraine. The West should also help fashion an economic rescue plan for Ukraine funded jointly by the EU, the International Monetary Fund, Russia, and the United States—a proposal that Moscow should welcome, given its interest in having a prosperous and stable Ukraine on its western flank. And the West should considerably limit its social-engineering efforts inside Ukraine. It is time to put an end to Western support for another Orange Revolution. Nevertheless, U.S. and European leaders should encourage Ukraine to respect minority rights, especially the language rights of its Russian speakers.

Some may argue that changing policy toward Ukraine at this late date would seriously damage U.S. credibility around the world. There would undoubtedly be certain costs, but the costs of continuing a misguided strategy would be much greater. Furthermore, other countries are likely to respect a state that learns from its mistakes and ultimately devises a policy that deals effectively with the problem at hand. That option is clearly open to the United States.

One also hears the claim that Ukraine has the right to determine whom it wants to ally with and the Russians have no right to prevent Kiev from joining the West. This is a dangerous way for Ukraine to think about its foreign policy choices. The sad truth is that might often makes right when great-power politics are at play. Abstract rights such as self-determination are largely meaningless when powerful states get into brawls with weaker states. Did Cuba have the right to form a military alliance with the Soviet Union during the Cold War? The United States certainly did not think so, and the Russians think the same way about Ukraine joining the West. It is in Ukraine's interest to understand these facts of life and tread carefully when dealing with its more powerful neighbor.

Even if one rejects this analysis, however, and believes that Ukraine has the right to petition to join the EU and NATO, the fact remains that the United States and its European allies have the right to reject these requests. There is no reason that the West has to accommodate Ukraine if it is bent on pursuing a wrong-headed foreign policy, especially if its defense is not a vital interest. Indulging the dreams of some Ukrainians is not worth the animosity and strife it will cause, especially for the Ukrainian people.

Of course, some analysts might concede that NATO handled relations with Ukraine poorly and yet still maintain that Russia constitutes an enemy that will only grow more formidable over time—and that the West therefore has no choice but to continue its present policy. But this viewpoint is badly mistaken. Russia is a declining power, and it will only get weaker with time. Even if Russia were a rising power, moreover, it would still make no sense to incorporate Ukraine into NATO. The reason is simple: the United States and its European allies do not consider Ukraine to be a core strategic interest, as their unwillingness to use military force to come to its aid has proved. It would therefore be the height of folly to create a new NATO member that the other members have no intention of defending. NATO has expanded in the past because liberals assumed the alliance would never have to honor its new security guarantees, but Russia's recent power play shows that granting Ukraine NATO membership could put Russia and the West on a collision course.

Sticking with the current policy would also complicate Western relations with Moscow on other issues. The United States needs Russia's assistance to withdraw U.S. equipment from Afghanistan through Russian territory, reach a nuclear agreement with Iran, and stabilize the situation in Syria. In fact, Moscow has helped Washington on all three of these issues in the past; in the summer of 2013, it was Putin who pulled Obama's chestnuts out of the fire by forging the deal under which Syria agreed to relinquish its chemical weapons, thereby avoiding the U.S. military strike that Obama had threatened. The United States will also someday need Russia's help containing a rising China. Current U.S. policy, however, is only driving Moscow and Beijing closer together.

The United States and its European allies now face a choice on Ukraine. They can continue their current policy, which will exacerbate hostilities with Russia and devastate Ukraine in the process—a scenario in which everyone would come out a loser. Or they can switch gears and work to create a prosperous but neutral Ukraine, one that does not threaten Russia and allows the West to repair its relations with Moscow. With that approach, all sides would win.

Faulty Powers

Who Started the Ukraine Crisis?

Michael McFaul; Stephen Sestanovich;
John J. Mearsheimer

FROM OUR NOVEMBER/
DECEMBER 2014 ISSUE

MOSCOW'S CHOICE

John Mearsheimer (*"Why the Ukraine Crisis Is the West's Fault,"*
September/ October 2014) is one of the most consistent and
persuasive theorists in the realist school of international relations, but his explanation of the crisis in Ukraine demonstrates
the limits of realpolitik. At best, Mearsheimer's brand of realism
explains only some aspects of U.S.-Russian relations over the last
30 years. And as a policy prescription, it can be irrational and
dangerous—as Russian President Vladimir Putin's embrace of it
demonstrates.

According to Mearsheimer, Russia has annexed Crimea and intervened in eastern Ukraine in response to NATO expansion,
which he calls "the taproot of the trouble." Russia's state-controlled
media have indeed pointed to the alliance's enlargement as an explanation for Putin's actions. But both Russian television coverage

MICHAEL MCFAUL is Professor of Political Science, Peter and Helen Bing
Senior Fellow at the Hoover Institution, and a Senior Fellow at the Freeman
Spogli Institute for International Studies, all at Stanford University. He served
as Special Assistant to the President on the National Security Council from
2009 to 2012 and U.S. Ambassador to Russia from 2012 to 2014.

STEPHEN SESTANOVICH is a Senior Fellow at the Council on Foreign Relations and a Professor at Columbia's School of International and Public Affairs,
and he was U.S. Ambassador-at-Large for the Former Soviet Union in 1997–
2001. He is the author of *Maximalist: America in the World From Truman to
Obama.*

and Mearsheimer's essay fail to explain why Russia kept its troops out of Ukraine for the decade-plus between NATO's expansion, which began in 1999, and the actual intervention in Ukraine in 2014. It's not that Russia was too weak: it launched two wars in Chechnya that required much more military might than the Crimean annexation did.

Even more difficult for Mearsheimer to explain is the so-called reset of U.S.-Russian relations, an era of cooperation that lasted from the spring of 2009 to January 2012. Both U.S. President Barack Obama and then Russian President Dmitry Medvedev agreed to moves that they considered in the national interest of their respective countries. The two leaders signed and ratified the New START treaty, voted to support the UN Security Council's most comprehensive set of sanctions against Iran ever, and vastly expanded the supply route for U.S. soldiers in Afghanistan that travels in part through Russia. They worked together to obtain Russian membership in the World Trade Organization, created a bilateral presidential commission to promote cooperation on everything from nuclear energy to counterterrorism, and put in place a more liberal visa regime. In 2010, polls showed that over 60 percent of Russians held a positive view of the United States.

Russia has pursued both cooperation and confrontation with the United States since this century began. Mearsheimer's single variable of NATO expansion can't explain both outcomes. For the real story, one needs to look past the factor that has stayed constant and focus on what has changed: Russian politics.

SOME STRATEGIST

Although realists prefer to focus on the state as the unit of analysis, for his explanation of the Ukraine crisis, Mearsheimer looks to individual leaders and their ideologies. He describes Putin as "a first-class strategist" who is armed with the correct analytic framework—that is, Mearsheimer's. "Putin and his compatriots have been thinking and acting according to realist dictates, whereas their Western counterparts have been adhering to liberal ideas about international politics," he writes. "The result is that the United States and its allies unknowingly provoked a major crisis over Ukraine."

By introducing leaders and their ideas into his analysis, Mearsheimer allows for the possibility that different statesmen guided by different ideologies might produce different foreign policies. Mearsheimer presumably believes that the United States and the world would be better off if U.S. leaders fully embraced his brand of realpolitik, whereas I think both would be better off if Putin and future Russian leaders embraced liberalism. But we don't have to dream about what this counterfactual might look like; we witnessed it during the Medvedev era.

In the first months of his presidency, Medvedev sounded very much like his realist mentor, Putin. He supported the Russian military intervention into Georgia and coined a strikingly realist term, "sphere of privileged interests," to assert Russia's hegemony in former Soviet territory. Obama rejected Medvedev's interpretation of realism. Meeting with Medvedev in April 2009 in London, Obama countered that the United States and Russia had many common interests, even in Russia's neighborhood.

At the time, the Obama administration was fighting desperately to keep open the U.S. military's Manas Air Base in Kyrgyzstan. Several weeks earlier, Kyrgyz President Kurmanbek Bakiyev had traveled to Moscow and received a pledge for $2 billion in economic assistance, and soon thereafter he announced his intention to close the base. With Medvedev, Obama acknowledged the balance-of-power politics that the Kremlin was playing, but then asked if closing the base was truly in Russia's national interest. After all, the U.S. soldiers flying through it were headed to Afghanistan to fight terrorists whom both the United States and Russia considered enemies. Keeping the base operating, Obama reasoned, was not a violation of Russia's "sphere of privileged interests" but a win-win outcome for both Washington and Moscow.

A realist would have rejected Obama's logic and pressed forward with closing the base—as Putin eventually did, earlier this year. In the months after the Obama-Medvedev meeting in 2009, however, the Kyrgyz government—with the Kremlin's tacit support—agreed to extend the U.S. government's basing rights. Medvedev gradually embraced Obama's framework of mutually beneficial relations. The progress made during the reset came about partly due to this shift in Russian foreign policy. Medvedev became so convinced about the utility of cooperation with the United States and support for international institutions that he even agreed to abstain from voting on (instead of vetoing) the UN Security Council resolutions authorizing the use of force against Muammar al-Qaddafi's regime in Libya in 2011—hardly behavior consistent with realism. After his final meeting with Obama in his capacity as Russian president, in South Korea in March 2012, Medvedev told the press that the reset was "an extremely useful exercise." "We probably enjoyed the best level of relations between the United States and Russia during those three years than ever during the previous decades," he said.

What he did not mention was NATO expansion. In fact, in the five years that I served in the Obama administration, I attended almost every meeting Obama held with Putin and Medvedev, and for three of those years, while working at the White House, I listened in on every phone conversation, and I cannot remember NATO expansion ever coming up. Even months before Putin's annexation of Crimea, I cannot recall a single major statement from a senior Russian official warning about the dangerous consequences of NATO expansion. The reason is simple: for the previous several years, NATO was not expanding eastward.

Other realist critics of U.S. policy make a similar mistake when they argue that the Obama administration showed weakness toward the Kremlin, inviting Putin to take advantage of it. Like Mearsheimer's analysis, this argument is fuzzy on causation. It's not clear, for example, how refusing to sign the New start treaty or declining to press Russia to vote for sanctions against Iran would have reduced the odds that Russia would have invaded Ukraine. Moreover, after 2012, Obama changed course and pursued a more confrontational approach in reaction to Putin's behavior. He abandoned missile defense talks, signed no new arms control treaties, levied sanctions against Russian human rights offenders, and canceled the summit with Putin scheduled for September 2013. Going further than what President George W. Bush did after Russia's 2008 invasion of Georgia, Obama worked with U.S. allies to impose sanctions on individual Russian leaders and companies. He shored up NATO's security commitments, provided assistance to Ukraine, and framed the West's response to Russia's aggression as necessary to preserve international norms and defend democratic values.

These moves can hardly be described as weak or unrealistic. Nonetheless, they failed to deter Russia's recent aggression, just as all U.S. presidents since 1956 have failed to deter Russian interventions in eastern Europe and Afghanistan. Realists who criticize Obama for failing to stand up to Putin must make a persuasive argument about how a different policy could have led to a different outcome. There is only one alternative policy that could have plausibly given Russia pause: granting NATO membership to Ukraine many years ago. But making that counterfactual convincing requires revising a lot of history. For the last several years, neither the Ukrainian government nor NATO members wanted Kiev to join the alliance anytime soon. Even before Viktor Yanukovych's election as president in 2010, Ukrainian leaders were not pressing for membership, and nor were the Ukrainian people.

THE REAL STORY

Russian foreign policy did not grow more aggressive in response to U.S. policies; it changed as a result of Russian internal political dynamics. The shift began when Putin and his regime came under attack for the first time ever. After Putin announced that he would run for a third presidential term, Russia held parliamentary elections in December 2011 that were just as fraudulent as previous elections. But this time, new technologies and social media—including smartphones with video cameras, Twitter, Facebook, and the Russian social network VKontakte—helped expose the government's wrongdoing and turn out protests on a scale not seen since the final months of the Soviet Union. Disapproval of voter fraud quickly morphed into discontent with Putin's return to the Kremlin. Some opposition leaders even called for revolutionary change.

Putin despised the protesters for their ingratitude. In his view, he had made them rich. How could they turn on him now? But he also feared them, especially in the wake of the "color revolutions" in eastern Europe (especially the 2004 Orange Revolution in Ukraine) and the Arab Spring. In an effort to mobilize his electoral base and discredit the opposition, Putin recast the United States as an enemy. Suddenly, state-controlled media were portraying the United States as fomenting unrest inside Russia. The Russian press accused me of being an agent sent by Obama to lead another color revolution. U.S. policy toward Russia hardly shifted at all between the parliamentary vote and Putin's reelection. Yet by the time Putin was inaugurated, in May 2012, even a casual observer of Putin's speeches or Russian television would have thought that the Cold War was back on.

Some observers of Russian politics hoped that this onslaught of anti-American propaganda would subside after the Russian presidential election was over. Many—including me—assumed that the Medvedev-Putin job swap would produce only minor changes in Russia's foreign policy, since Putin had remained the paramount decision-maker when Medvedev was president. But over time, it became clear that Putin conceived of Russia's national interest differently from how Medvedev did. Unlike Medvedev, Putin tended to frame competition with the United States in zero-sum terms. To sustain his legitimacy at home, Putin continued to need the United States as an adversary. He also genuinely believed that the United States represented a sinister force in world affairs.

Then came the upheaval in Ukraine. In November 2013, Ukrainians took to the streets after Yanukovych declined to sign an association agreement with the EU. The U.S. government played no role in sparking the protests, but it did prod both Yanukovych and opposition leaders to agree to a transitional plan, which both sides signed on February 21, 2014. Washington also had nothing to do with Yanukovych's surprising decision to flee Ukraine the next day.

Putin interpreted these events differently, blaming the United States for the demonstrations, the failure of the February 21 agreement, and the subsequent change of government, which he called a coup. Putin's ideology compelled him to frame these events as a struggle between the United States and Russia. Constrained by this analytic framework, he reacted unilaterally in a way that he believed tilted the balance of power in his favor, annexing Crimea and supporting armed mercenaries in eastern Ukraine. He was not reacting to NATO's long-ago expansion.

PUTIN'S LOSS

It is too early to judge whether Putin's particular brand of realism is rational in terms of Russia's national interest. So far, however, the gains have been limited. His allegedly pragmatic and realist actions in Ukraine have only served to forge a stronger, more unified, and more pro-Western identity among Ukrainians. They have guaranteed that Ukraine will never join his most prized project, the planned Eurasian Economic Union, and have instead pushed the country toward the EU. Meanwhile, Belarus and Kazakhstan have turned into nervous, less enthusiastic partners in the Eurasian Economic Union. At the same time, Putin has strengthened NATO, weakened the Russian economy, and undermined Moscow's international reputation as a champion of sovereignty and noninterference.

This crisis is not about Russia, NATO, and realism but about Putin and his unconstrained, erratic adventurism. Whether you label its approach realist or liberal, the challenge for the West is how to deal with such behavior forcefully enough to block it but prudently enough to keep matters from escalating dramatically.

HOW THE WEST HAS WON

The United States has handled its relations with Russia so badly, John Mearsheimer argues, that it, not Vladimir Putin, should be held responsible for the crisis in Ukraine. By trying to get Ukraine into NATO, he writes, Western governments challenged Russia's core security interests. The Kremlin was bound to push back. Meanwhile, silly idealism kept U.S. and European leaders from recognizing the trouble they were creating.

To see what's wrong with this critique, one can start by comparing it with Mearsheimer's 1993 *Foreign Affairs* article, "The Case for a Ukrainian Nuclear Deterrent." Back then, Mearsheimer was already worrying about a war between Russia and Ukraine, which he said would be "a disaster." But he did not finger U.S. policy as the source of the problem. "Russia," Mearsheimer wrote, "has dominated an unwilling and angry Ukraine for more than two centuries, and has attempted to crush Ukraine's sense of self-identity." Given this history, creating a stable relationship between the two countries was bound to be hard. "Hypernationalism," Mearsheimer feared, would make the situation even more unmanageable. In 1993, his assessment of the situation (if not his policy prescriptions) was correct. It should serve as a reminder that today's aggressive Russian policy was in place long before the mistaken Western policies that Mearsheimer says explain it.

The prospect of NATO membership for Ukraine may, of course, have made a bad problem much worse. In 2008, Mearsheimer points out, NATO declared that Ukraine would at some point join the alliance. But he does not acknowledge what happened next. For more than half a decade, nearly all Ukrainian politicians—not just pro-Russian ones such as Viktor Yanukovych—steered clear of the issue. They recognized that NATO membership lacked strong domestic support and, if mishandled, could threaten national unity. NATO itself put the matter aside. Admitting Ukraine remained a pet project for a few members of the alliance, but most were opposed, many of them implacably so. The Obama administration, for its part, paid no attention to the subject, and the issue virtually disappeared.

That changed, Mearsheimer claims, with the fall of Yanukovych. Mearsheimer endorses Putin's label of that event as a "coup": a

Western-supported provocation that reignited Moscow's fears and justified an aggressive policy. But the facts do not support this interpretation. Few elected presidents have lost their legitimacy as quickly and fully as Yanukovych did. At every step during the "Euromaidan" protests, he kept the confrontation going by resorting to force. In February 2014, after police killed scores of demonstrators in downtown Kiev, the whole country turned against him, effectively ending his political career. Parliament removed him by a unanimous vote, in which every deputy of his own party participated. This is not what anyone has ever meant by the word "coup."

Yanukovych's fall was a historic event, but it did not, despite Russian claims, revive Ukraine's candidacy for NATO membership. Ukrainian politicians and officials said again and again that this issue was not on the agenda. Nor was the large Russian naval base in Crimea at risk, no matter the feverish charges of Russian commentators. That Putin picked up this argument—and accused "fascists" of having taken over Ukraine—had less to do with Russia's national security than his desire to rebound from political humiliation. Moscow had publicly urged Yanukovych to crack down hard on the protesters. When the Ukrainian leader obliged, his presidency collapsed, and with it Russia's entire Ukraine policy. Putin's seizure of Crimea was first and foremost an attempt to recover from his own egregious mistakes.

This sorry record makes it hard to credit Mearsheimer's description of Putin as "a first-class strategist." Yes, Russian aggression boosted Putin's poll numbers. But success in Crimea was followed by a series of gross miscalculations—about the extent of separatist support in eastern Ukraine, the capacities of the Ukrainian military, the possibility of keeping Russian interference hidden, the West's ability to agree on sanctions, and the reaction of European leaders who had once sympathized with Russia. And all of this for what? Putin cultivates a mystique of cool, KGB professionalism, and the image has often served him well. But the Ukraine crisis has revealed a different style of decision-making. Putin made impulsive decisions that subordinated Russia's national interest to his own personal political motives. He has not acted like a sober realist.

CHALLENGE AND RESPONSE

Even if Putin is to blame for the current crisis, it might still be possible to find fault with U.S. policy of the past two decades. There is, after all, no doubt that Russians resented NATO enlargement and their country's diminished international standing after the Cold War. For Mearsheimer, the West needlessly stoked this resentment. As he sees it, once the Soviet Union collapsed, Russia was simply too inconsequential to be worth containing, since it was "a declining great power with an aging population and a one-dimensional economy." Today, he calls its army "mediocre." Enlarging NATO was a solution to a problem that didn't exist.

This would be a compelling case but for one thing: in the early 1990s, Mearsheimer himself saw the post–Cold War world in much more menacing terms. Back then, no one knew what demons would be let loose by the end of East-West competition. Germany, just reunified, might once more go the way of militarism. Yugoslavia was undergoing a bloody breakup. Unscrupulous political leaders had been able to revive eastern Europe's many ancient hatreds. Add to this the risk that Russia itself, once it regained its strength, might threaten the independence of its neighbors, and it was not hard to imagine a Europe of severe turbulence.

Mearsheimer no longer mentions these problems, but at the time, he saw them for what they were. In a much-read 1990 *Atlantic Monthly* article, he predicted that we would all soon "miss the Cold War." To preserve the peace, he even proposed a set of extreme countermeasures, such as letting Moscow keep its large army in central Europe and encouraging Germany and Ukraine to acquire nuclear weapons. Today, these initiatives seem outlandish and otherworldly, to say the least, but the problems they aimed to solve were not imaginary.

Mearsheimer has long ridiculed the idea that, as he describes in his recent *Foreign Affairs* article, "Europe can be kept whole and free on the basis of such liberal principles as the rule of law, economic interdependence, and democracy." In his ire, however, he misses something fundamental. The goals of Western policy have been just as visionary and idealistic as he says, but the means employed to achieve them—at least by U.S. leaders, if not always by their European counterparts—have been far more traditional. They have been the medicine that a realist doctor would have prescribed.

The United States has defended its stake in a stable post–Cold War European order not through airy appeals to shared values but through the regular and effective use of old-fashioned American power. President George H. W. Bush, intending to limit the independence of German foreign policy, demanded a reunification deal that kept Germany within NATO. President Bill Clinton, believing that the Balkan wars of the 1990s were undermining U.S. power and credibility in Europe, twice used military force to stop Serbia under President Slobodan Milosevic. That President George W. Bush continued to take new eastern European democracies into NATO did not mean Washington believed that democracy alone would sustain the peace. It meant Washington believed that an enduring liberal order needed the anchor of U.S. commitment. (You might even say it meant U.S. policymakers did not in fact believe that democracy alone assures peace.)

No one, least of all Mearsheimer, should be surprised to discover that power calculations undergirded U.S. foreign policy. In his 2001 book, *The Tragedy of Great Power Politics*, he explained that politicians and policymakers in liberal democratic states often justify hardheaded actions in highfalutin language. Now, however, he takes everything that political leaders say—whether Obama's pieties or Putin's lies—at face value.

The resulting analysis makes it much harder to see whose policies are working, and what to do next. Mearsheimer seems to take it for granted that Putin's challenge proves the complete failure of U.S. strategy. But the mere fact that Russia has a leader bent on conquest is not by itself an indictment of the United States. Putin is certainly not the first such Russian leader, and he may not be the last. Nor are Ukraine's current agonies, as acute and unnecessary as they are, the best way to measure what nato enlargement has accomplished. Two decades of U.S. policy have both stabilized Europe and narrowed the scope of the current crisis. Had NATO not grown to its present size and borders, Russia's conflict with Ukraine would be far more dangerous than what is occurring today. Western leaders would be in a state of near panic as they tried to figure out, in the middle of a confrontation, which eastern European countries deserved security guarantees and which did not. At a moment of sudden tension, they would be obliged to improvise. Finding the right middle ground between recklessness and acquiescence would be a matter of guesswork, with unpredictable life-and-death results.

CALMING EUROPE

The addition of so many new NATO members in recent years does mean that the alliance needs to think carefully about how to implement the commitments it has made. But the job of promoting security in eastern Europe has been made much easier because a basic strategic framework is already in place. Ironically, even Putin, for all his complaining, benefits. Despite the rude jolt of his aggression against Ukraine, Western governments are less frightened than they would be without the comfort of a larger NATO and the relatively stable European order that U.S. policy has created. Putin faces less push-back today in part because the United States succeeded in solving the problems of the 1990s.

In proposing to turn Ukraine into "a neutral buffer between NATO and Russia," Mearsheimer offers a solution to the current crisis that ignores its real origins and may even make it worse. He is on solid enough ground when he reminds readers that Ukraine has no inherent "right" to join NATO. But good strategy doesn't look only at rights and wrongs; it looks at consequences. The best reason not to push for Ukraine's entry into NATO has always been to avoid tearing the country apart. By forcing Ukraine to repudiate a mere free-trade agreement with Europe last fall, Putin brought on the most extreme turmoil Ukraine has seen in 20 years of independence. Now that the world has seen the results of this little experiment, why should anyone think that declaring Ukraine a permanent gray area of international politics would calm the country down?

Ukraine has not been—and is not—ready for NATO membership. Only Putin has forced this issue onto the agenda. The immediate goal of prudent statesmen should be to figure out a way to hold Ukraine together. If the great powers impose or foreclose its future, they may deepen its present turmoil. The best way to avoid an escalation of radical political confrontation inside Ukraine is not to resolve the big geopolitical questions but to defer them.

Mearsheimer's real subject is, of course, not Ukraine but U.S. foreign policy. After the exertions of the past decade, some retrenchment was inevitable. That does not mean, however, that Washington was wrong to choose an ambitious and activist policy in Europe after the Cold War, or that it should not move toward a more ambitious and activist one now. In *The Tragedy of Great Power Politics*, Mearsheimer wrote that it was "misguided" for a state to "pass up an opportunity to be the hegemon in the system because it thought it already had sufficient power to survive." He may have forgotten his own advice, but Washington, in its confused and halting way, has usually followed it. Even today, the West is better off because it did.

MEARSHEIMER REPLIES

It is not surprising that Michael McFaul and Stephen Sestanovich disagree with my account of what caused the Ukraine crisis. Both the policies they helped frame and execute while in the U.S. government and their responses to my article exemplify the liberal foreign policy consensus that helped cause the crisis in the first place. Accordingly, they challenge my claims about the West's role, mostly by suggesting that I regard NATO expansion as the sole cause of the crisis. McFaul, for example, maintains that my "single variable of NATO expansion" cannot explain the ebb and flow of recent U.S.-Russian relations. Both also claim that the alliance's growth was a nonissue after 2008.

But McFaul and Sestanovich misrepresent my core argument. I did call NATO expansion "the central element of a larger strategy to move Ukraine out of Russia's orbit and integrate it into the West." Yet I also emphasized that the strategy had two other "critical elements": EU expansion and democracy promotion. My essay makes clear that NATO enlargement did not directly cause the crisis, which began in November 2013 and continues to this day. It was EU expansion coupled with the February 22, 2014, coup that ignited the fire. Still, what I called "the West's triple package of policies," which included making Ukraine part of NATO, provided fuel for it.

The notion that the issue of NATO membership for Ukraine, as Sestanovich puts it, "virtually disappeared" after 2008 is also false. No Western leader publicly questioned the alliance's 2008 declaration that Georgia and Ukraine "will become members of NATO." Sestanovich downplays that push, writing, "Admitting Ukraine remained a pet project for a few members of the alliance, but most were opposed, many of them implacably so." What he does not say, however, is that the United States was one of those members backing that pet project, and Washington still wields enormous influence within the alliance. And even if some members were opposed to bringing in Ukraine, Moscow could not count on the naysayers to prevail forever.

Furthermore, the association agreement that the EU was pushing Ukraine to sign in 2013 was not just "a mere free-trade agreement," as Sestanovich calls it; it also had an important security dimension. The document proposed that all parties "promote gradual convergence on foreign and security matters with the aim of Ukraine's ever-deeper involvement in the European security area" and called for "taking full and timely advantage of all diplomatic and military channels between the Parties." This certainly sounds like a backdoor to NATO membership, and no prudent Russian leader would interpret it any other way. McFaul and Sestanovich may believe that expanding NATO was genuinely off the table after 2008, but that is not how Vladimir Putin and his colleagues saw it.

To argue that Russia's reaction to NATO expansion was based on "resentment," as Sestanovich does, is to trivialize the country's motives. Fear is at the root of Russia's opposition to the prospect of Ukraine becoming a Western bastion on its border. Great powers always worry about the balance of power in their neighborhoods and push back when other great powers march up to their doorsteps. This is why the United States adopted the Monroe Doctrine in the early nineteenth century and why it has repeatedly used military force and covert action to shape political events in the Western Hemisphere. When the Soviet Union placed missiles in Cuba in 1962, U.S. President John F. Kennedy, risking a nuclear war, insisted that they be removed. Security fears, not resentment, drove his conduct.

The same logic applies to Russia. As its leaders have made clear on countless occasions, they will not tolerate Ukraine's entry into NATO. That outcome scares them, as it would scare anyone in Russia's shoes, and fearful great powers often pursue aggressive policies. The failure to understand that Russian thinking about NATO enlargement was motivated by fear—a misreading McFaul and Sestanovich still embrace—helped precipitate the present crisis.

COOPERATION AND CONFLICT

McFaul claims that I cannot explain the periods of cooperation and confrontation between Russia and the West whereas he has a compelling explanation for both. This criticism follows from his claim that I have a monocausal argument based on NATO expansion and that this single factor "can't explain both outcomes." But I never argued that NATO expansion, which began in the late 1990s, led to a state of constant crisis. Indeed, I noted that Russia has cooperated with the West on a number of important issues—Afghanistan, Iran, Syria—but that Western policies were making it increasingly difficult to sustain those good relations. The actual crisis, of course, did not erupt until the February 22, 2014, coup.

Two points are in order regarding the coup itself. First, Sestanovich is wrong to suggest that Ukrainian President Viktor Yanukovych was removed from office legitimately. In a city racked by violence between protesters and government forces, on February 21 a deal was struck with Yanukovych to hold new elections that would surely have removed him from power. But many of the protesters opposed the agreement, insisting that Yanukovych step down immediately. On February 22, armed elements of the opposition, including some fascists, occupied parliament and the main presidential offices. That same day, the legislature held a vote to oust Yanukovych that did not satisfy the Ukrainian constitution's requirements for impeachment. No wonder he fled the country, fearing for his life.

Second, McFaul implies that Washington had nothing to do with the coup. "The U.S. government played no role in sparking the protests," he writes, "but it did prod both Yanukovych and opposition leaders to agree to a transitional plan." McFaul fails to mention the considerable evidence I presented showing that the United States was encouraging the opposition to Yanukovych before and during the protests. Such actions included the National Endowment for Democracy's decision to ramp up support for anti-Yanukovych groups and the active participation of top U.S. officials (such as Victoria Nuland, the assistant secretary of state for European and Eurasian affairs) in the public protests in Kiev.

These events alarmed Putin, not only because they threatened his relations with Ukraine but also because he may well have thought that the Obama administration was bent on overthrowing him, too. As I noted in my essay, Carl Gershman, the president of the National Endowment for Democracy, said in September 2013 that "Ukraine's choice to join Europe" would promote Russian democracy and might eventually topple Putin from power. And when McFaul was the U.S. ambassador in Moscow, he openly promoted democracy in Russia, behavior that led the Russian press to accuse him of, in his words, "being an agent sent by Obama to lead another color revolution." Such fears may have been exaggerated, but imagine how U.S. leaders would react if representatives of a powerful foreign country were trying to alter the United States' political order.

McFaul argues that differences between individual leaders explain Russia's alternating policies of cooperation and confrontation: everything is hunky-dory when Dmitry Medvedev is president, but trouble comes when Putin takes charge. The problem with this argument is that these two leaders hardly disagree about Russian foreign policy, which is why Putin is widely regarded as Medvedev's "realist mentor," to use McFaul's words. Medvedev was president when Russia went to war against Georgia in 2008, and he has fully supported Putin's actions over Ukraine this year. In September, he went so far as to criticize Putin for not responding more forcefully to Western sanctions on Russia. And even during the "reset," Medvedev complained bitterly about NATO's "endless enlargement," as he put it in a 2010 interview.

There is a better explanation for Russia's oscillating relations with the West. When the United States and its allies take note of Moscow's concerns, as they did during the early years of the reset, crises are averted and Russia cooperates on matters of mutual concern. When the West ignores Moscow's interests, as it did in the lead-up to the Ukraine crisis, confrontation reigns. Putin openly welcomed the reset, telling Obama in July 2009, "With you, we link all our hopes for the furtherance of relations between our two countries." And two months later, when Obama abandoned plans to put missile defense systems in the Czech Republic and Poland, Putin praised the decision, saying, "I very much hope that this very right and brave decision will be followed by others." It is unsurprising that when Putin returned to the presidency in May 2012, McFaul, then U.S. ambassador to Russia, said that he expected the reset to continue. In short, Medvedev's replacement by Putin was not the watershed event McFaul portrays it as—and had Medvedev remained president, he would probably have reacted to events in Ukraine the same way Putin has.

Sestanovich claims that "today's aggressive Russian policy was in place" in the early 1990s and that the U.S. response was grounded in "power calculations." But the evidence suggests that NATO enlargement does not represent a realist policy. Russia was in no position to take the offensive in the 1990s, and although its economy and military improved somewhat in the next decade, hardly anyone in the West thought it was seriously at risk of invading its neighbors—especially Ukraine—before the February 22 coup. Not surprisingly, U.S. leaders rarely invoked the threat of Russian aggression to justify expanding NATO; instead, they emphasized the benefits of expanding the zone of democratic peace eastward.

Indeed, although Sestanovich now maintains that "Russia has a leader bent on conquest," there is no evidence that this was his view before the current crisis. For example, in an interview about the ongoing protests in Ukraine published on December 4, 2013—roughly three months before Russia took Crimea—he gave no indication that he thought Putin was set to invade Ukraine (or any other country) or that NATO expansion was necessary to contain Russia. On the contrary, when discussing the alliance's moves eastward with a Voice of America reporter in 2004, Sestanovich suggested that Russian objections were little more than political posturing. "Russians probably feel that they need to object to this in order to indicate that they are a serious country that cannot be pushed around," he said.

Sestanovich's views reflected the liberal consensus at the time, which saw NATO expansion as benign. "Most analysts agree the enlargement of NATO and the EU should not pose a long-term threat to Russian interests," wrote that same Voice of America reporter, summarizing the positions of the various experts he had interviewed. "They point out that having stable and secure neighbors may increase stability and prosperity in Russia, as well as help overcome old Cold War fears and encourage former Soviet satellites to engage Russia in a more positive, cooperative way."

HOW IT ENDS

McFaul and Sestanovich maintain that Putin's behavior over Ukraine has been wrong-headed and counterproductive. It is too soon to know how this saga will end, but there is good reason to think that Putin will achieve his primary aim—preventing Ukraine from becoming a Western bulwark. If so, he wins, although there is no question that Russia will have paid a steep price in the process.

The real losers, however, will be the Ukrainian people. Sestanovich writes that "the best reason not to push for Ukraine's entry into NATO has always been to avoid tearing the country apart." He is correct. But the policies he and McFaul support have done just that.

A Broken Promise?

What the West Really Told Moscow About NATO Expansion

Mary Elise Sarotte

FROM OUR SEPTEMBER/
OCTOBER 2014 ISSUE

Twenty-five years ago this November, an East German Politburo member bungled the announcement of what were meant to be limited changes to travel regulations, thereby inspiring crowds to storm the border dividing East and West Berlin. The result was the iconic moment marking the point of no return in the end of the Cold War: the fall of the Berlin Wall. In the months that followed, the United States, the Soviet Union, and West Germany engaged in fateful negotiations over the withdrawal of Soviet troops and the reunification of Germany. Although these talks eventually resulted in German reunification on October 3, 1990, they also gave rise to a later, bitter dispute between Russia and the West. What, exactly, had been agreed about the future of NATO? Had the United States formally promised the Soviet Union that the alliance would not expand eastward as part of the deal?

Even more than two decades later, the dispute refuses to go away. Russian diplomats regularly assert that Washington made just such a promise in exchange for the Soviet troop withdrawal from East Germany—and then betrayed that promise as NATO

MARY ELISE SAROTTE is Dean's Professor of History at the University of Southern California, a Visiting Professor at Harvard University, and the author of *The Collapse: The Accidental Opening of the Berlin Wall*. This essay is adapted from the afterword to the updated edition of her book *1989: The Struggle to Create Post-Cold War Europe* (Princeton University Press, 2014).

added 12 eastern European countries in three subsequent rounds of enlargement. Writing in this magazine earlier this year, the Russian foreign policy thinker Alexander Lukin accused successive U.S. presidents of "forgetting the promises made by Western leaders to Mikhail Gorbachev after the unification of Germany—most notably that they would not expand NATO eastward." Indeed, Russian President Vladimir Putin's aggressive actions in Georgia in 2008 and Ukraine in 2014 were fueled in part by his ongoing resentment about what he sees as the West's broken pact over NATO expansion. But U.S. policymakers and analysts insist that such a promise never existed. In a 2009 *Washington Quarterly* article, for example, the scholar Mark Kramer assured readers not only that Russian claims were a complete "myth" but also that "the issue never came up during the negotiations on German reunification."

Now that increasing numbers of formerly secret documents from 1989 and 1990 have made their way into the public domain, historians can shed new light on this controversy. The evidence demonstrates that contrary to the conventional wisdom in Washington, the issue of NATO's future in not only East Germany but also eastern Europe arose soon after the Berlin Wall opened, as early as February 1990. U.S. officials, working closely with West German leaders, hinted to Moscow during negotiations that month that the alliance might not expand, not even to the eastern half of a soon-to-be-reunited Germany.

Documents also show that the United States, with the help of West Germany, soon pressured Gorbachev into allowing Germany to reunify, without making any kind of written promise about the alliance's future plans. Put simply, there was never a formal deal, as Russia alleges—but U.S. and West German officials briefly implied that such a deal might be on the table, and in return they received a "green light" to commence the process of German reunification. The dispute over this sequence of events has distorted relations between Washington and Moscow ever since.

GETTING THE GREEN LIGHT

Western leaders quickly realized that the fall of the Berlin Wall had brought seemingly long-settled issues of European security once again into play. By the beginning of 1990, the topic of NATO's future role was coming up frequently during confidential conversations among U.S. President George H. W. Bush; James Baker, the U.S. secretary of state; Helmut Kohl, the West German chancellor; Hans-Dietrich Genscher, the West German foreign minister; and Douglas Hurd, the British foreign minister.

According to documents from the West German foreign ministry, for example, Genscher told Hurd on February 6 that Gorbachev would want to rule out the prospect of NATO's future expansion not only to East Germany but also to eastern Europe. Genscher suggested that the alliance should issue a public statement saying that "NATO does not intend to expand its territory to the East." "Such a statement must refer not just to [East Germany], but rather be of a general nature," he added. "For example, the Soviet Union needs the security of knowing that Hungary, if it has a change of government, will not become part of the Western Alliance." Genscher urged that NATO discuss the matter immediately, and Hurd agreed.

Three days later, in Moscow, Baker talked NATO with Gorbachev directly. During their meeting, Baker took handwritten notes of his own remarks, adding stars next to the key words: "End result: Unified Ger. anchored in a ´changed (polit.) NATO—´whose juris. would not move ´eastward!" Baker's notes appear to be the only place such an assurance was written down on February 9, and they raise an interesting question. If Baker's "end result" was that the jurisdiction of NATO's collective-defense provision would not move eastward, did that mean it would not move into the territory of former East Germany after reunification?

In answering that question, it is fortunate for posterity's sake that Genscher and Kohl were just about to visit Moscow themselves. Baker left behind with the West German ambassador in Moscow a secret letter for Kohl that has been preserved in the

German archives. In it, Baker explained that he had put the crucial statement to Gorbachev in the form of a question: "Would you prefer to see a unified Germany outside of NATO, independent and with no U.S. forces," he asked, presumably framing the option of an untethered Germany in a way that Gorbachev would find unattractive, "or would you prefer a unified Germany to be tied to NATO, with assurances that NATO's jurisdiction would not shift one inch eastward from its present position?"

Baker's phrasing of the second, more attractive option meant that NATO's jurisdiction would not even extend to East Germany, since NATO's "present position" in February 1990 remained exactly where it had been throughout the Cold War: with its eastern edge on the line still dividing the two Germanies. In other words, a united Germany would be, de facto, half in and half out of the alliance. According to Baker, Gorbachev responded, "Certainly any extension of the zone of NATO would be unacceptable." In Baker's view, Gorbachev's reaction indicated that "NATO in its current zone might be acceptable."

After receiving their own report on what had happened in Moscow, however, staff members on the National Security Council back in Washington felt that such a solution would be unworkable as a practical matter. How could NATO's jurisdiction apply to only half of a country? Such an outcome was neither desirable nor, they suspected, necessary. As a result, the National Security Council put together a letter to Kohl under Bush's name. It arrived just before Kohl departed for his own trip to Moscow.

Instead of implying that NATO would not move eastward, as Baker had done, this letter proposed a "special military status for what is now the territory of [East Germany]." Although the letter did not define exactly what the special status would entail, the implication was clear: all of Germany would be in the alliance, but to make it easier for Moscow to accept this development, some kind of face-saving regulations would apply to its eastern region (restrictions on the activities of certain kinds of NATO troops, as it turned out).

Kohl thus found himself in a complicated position as he prepared to meet with Gorbachev on February 10, 1990. He had received two letters, one on either end of his flight from West Germany to the Soviet Union, the first from Bush and the second from Baker, and the two contained different wording on the same issue. Bush's letter suggested that NATO's border would begin moving eastward; Baker's suggested that it would not.

According to records from Kohl's office, the chancellor chose to echo Baker, not Bush, since Baker's softer line was more likely to produce the results that Kohl wanted: permission from Moscow to start reunifying Germany. Kohl thus assured Gorbachev that "naturally NATO could not expand its territory to the current territory of [East Germany]." In parallel talks, Genscher delivered the same message to his Soviet counterpart, Eduard Shevardnadze, saying, "for us, it stands firm: NATO will not expand itself to the East."

As with Baker's meeting with Gorbachev, no written agreement emerged. After hearing these repeated assurances, Gorbachev gave West Germany what Kohl later called "the green light" to begin creating an economic and monetary union between East and West Germany—the first step of reunification. Kohl held a press conference immediately to lock in this gain. As he recalled in his memoirs, he was so overjoyed that he couldn't sleep that night, and so instead went for a long, cold walk through Red Square.

BRIBING THE SOVIETS OUT

But Kohl's phrasing would quickly become heresy among the key Western decision-makers. Once Baker got back to Washington, in mid-February 1990, he fell in line with the National Security Council's view and adopted its position. From then on, members of Bush's foreign policy team exercised strict message discipline, making no further remarks about NATO holding at the 1989 line.

Kohl, too, brought his rhetoric in line with Bush's, as both U.S. and West German transcripts from the two leaders' February 24–25 summit at Camp David show. Bush made his feelings about compromising with Moscow clear to Kohl: "To hell with that!" he said. "We prevailed, they didn't. We can't let the Soviets clutch victory from the jaws of defeat." Kohl argued that he and Bush would have to find a way to placate Gorbachev, predicting, "It will come down in the end to a question of cash." Bush pointedly noted that West Germany had "deep pockets." A straightforward strategy thus arose: as Robert Gates, then U.S. deputy national security adviser, later explained it, the goal was to "bribe the Soviets out." And West Germany would pay the bribe.

In April, Bush spelled out this thinking in a confidential telegram to French President François Mitterrand. U.S. officials worried that the Kremlin might try to outmaneuver them by allying with the United Kingdom or France, both of which were also still occupying Berlin and, given their past encounters with a hostile Germany, potentially had reason to share the Soviets' unease about reunification. So Bush emphasized his top priorities to Mitterrand: that a united Germany enjoy full membership in NATO, that allied forces remain in a united Germany even after Soviet troops withdraw, and that NATO continue to deploy both nuclear and conventional weapons in the region. He warned Mitterrand that no other organization could "replace NATO as the guarantor of Western security and stability." He continued: "Indeed, it is difficult to visualize how a European collective security arrangement including Eastern Europe, and perhaps even the Soviet Union, would have the capability to deter threats to Western Europe."

Bush was making it clear to Mitterrand that the dominant security organization in a post–Cold War Europe had to remain NATO—and not any kind of pan-European alliance. As it happened, the next month, Gorbachev proposed just such a pan-European arrangement, one in which a united Germany would join both NATO and the Warsaw Pact, thus creating one massive security institution. Gorbachev even raised the idea of having the Soviet Union join NATO. "You say that NATO is not directed against us, that it is simply a security structure that is adapting to new realities," Gorbachev told Baker in May, according to Soviet records. "Therefore, we propose to join NATO." Baker refused to consider such a notion, replying dismissively, "Pan-European security is a dream."

Throughout 1990, U.S. and West German diplomats successfully countered such proposals, partly by citing Germany's right to determine its alliance partners itself. As they did so, it became clear that Bush and Kohl had guessed correctly: Gorbachev would, in fact, eventually bow to Western preferences, as long as he was compensated. Put bluntly, he needed the cash. In May 1990, Jack Matlock, the U.S. ambassador to Moscow, reported that Gorbachev was starting to look "less like a man in control and more [like] an embattled leader." The "signs of crisis," he wrote in a cable from Moscow, "are legion: Sharply rising crime rates, proliferating anti-regime demonstrations, burgeoning separatist movements, deteriorating economic performance . . . and a slow, uncertain transfer of power from party to state and from the center to the periphery."

Moscow would have a hard time addressing these domestic problems without the help of foreign aid and credit, which meant that it might be willing to compromise. The question was whether West Germany could provide such assistance in a manner that would allow Gorbachev to avoid looking as though he was being bribed into accepting a reunified Germany in NATO with no meaningful restrictions on the alliance's movement eastward.

Kohl accomplished this difficult task in two bursts: first, in a bilateral meeting with Gorbachev in July 1990, and then, in a set of emotional follow-up phone calls in September 1990. Gorbachev ultimately gave his assent to a united Germany in NATO in exchange for face-saving measures, such as a four-year grace period for removing Soviet troops and some restrictions on both NATO troops and nuclear weapons on former East German territory. He also received 12 billion deutsch marks to construct housing for the withdrawing Soviet troops and another three billion in interest-free credit. What he did not receive were any formal guarantees against NATO expansion.

In August 1990, Saddam Hussein's invasion of Kuwait immediately pushed Europe down the White House's list of foreign policy priorities. Then, after Bush lost the 1992 presidential election to Bill Clinton, Bush's staff members had to vacate their offices earlier than they had expected. They appear to have communicated little with the incoming Clinton team. As a result, Clinton's staffers began their tenure with limited or no knowledge of what Washington and Moscow had discussed regarding NATO.

THE SEEDS OF A FUTURE PROBLEM

Contrary to the view of many on the U.S. side, then, the question of NATO expansion arose early and entailed discussions of expansion not only to East Germany but also to eastern Europe. But contrary to Russian allegations, Gorbachev never got the West to promise that it would freeze NATO's borders. Rather, Bush's senior advisers had a spell of internal disagreement in early February 1990, which they displayed to Gorbachev. By the time of the Camp David summit, however, all members of Bush's team, along with Kohl, had united behind an offer in which Gorbachev would receive financial assistance from West Germany—and little else—in exchange for allowing Germany to reunify and for allowing a united Germany to be part of NATO.

In the short run, the result was a win for the United States. U.S. officials and their West German counterparts had expertly outmaneuvered Gorbachev, extending NATO to East Germany and avoiding promises about the future of the alliance. One White House staffer under Bush, Robert Hutchings, ranked a dozen possible outcomes, from the "most congenial" (no restrictions at all on NATO as it moved into former East Germany) to the "most inimical" (a united Germany completely outside of NATO). In the end, the United States achieved an outcome somewhere between the best and the second best on the list. Rarely does one country win so much in an international negotiation.

But as Baker presciently wrote in his memoirs of his tenure as secretary of state, "Almost every achievement contains within its success the seeds of a future problem." By design, Russia was left on the periphery of a post–Cold War Europe. A young KGB officer serving in East Germany in 1989 offered his own recollection of the era in an interview a decade later, in which he remembered returning to Moscow full of bitterness at how "the Soviet Union had lost its position in Europe." His name was Vladimir Putin, and he would one day have the power to act on that bitterness.

Putin's Wager

Why the Kremlin Is Betting on Escalation and Isolation

Joshua Yaffa   AUGUST 6, 2014

After Malaysia Airlines flight MH17 was shot down over eastern Ukraine on July 17, a catastrophe almost certainly the work of Russian-backed rebels, the United States and the EU implemented new, wider-reaching sanctions. Russian President Vladimir Putin responded by redoubling his Ukraine policy. Rather than distancing itself from the militia groups, Moscow has stepped up its support, transferring arms, providing diplomatic cover, and even ordering Russian forces to fire on Ukrainian military targets across the border. Given the opportunity to abandon an increasingly costly policy, Putin has chosen to escalate.

In so doing, he is steering his country toward a period of prolonged isolation and economic difficulty. U.S. President Barack Obama suggested last week that Putin is behaving irrationally. "Objectively speaking, President Putin should want to resolve this diplomatically, to get these sanctions lifted," Obama said. There is a limit to what the United States can achieve, he added, when Putin and those around him are "ignoring what should be their long-term interests."

But those interests look very different from Moscow than they do from Washington. Putin and his close advisers may be cynical, but they are sincere in their cynicism. They see the West, and the United States in particular, as engaged in an unceasing effort to

JOSHUA YAFFA is a journalist based in Moscow, where he is a contributor to *The Economist*, among other publications.

weaken and fracture Russia. For them, Ukraine represents a red-line. Putin's suspicions of Western motives, dissatisfaction with the post–Cold War global order, and fears of a pro-Western Ukraine are parts of the same potent cocktail of grievance and paranoia. The best, if not the only, prophylactic is what Putin understands as "sovereignty." It is a concept that Putin warned his Security Council is "being washed out" by "ultimatums and sanctions." It is also, as Putin sees it, what Soviet Premier Mikhail Gorbachev let slip out from under him, leading to the disintegration of state power— and thus precisely what Putin is intent on preserving.

To Putin, sovereignty constitutes the essence of power. "Putin's motivating idea is that Russia's influence is preordained," said Sergey Utkin, the head of the Department of Strategic Assessment, part of the Russian Academy of Sciences. "It's a genuine conviction, a call, a challenge that must be answered in the country's policies." Were Putin to back down over Ukraine, even after the attack on MH17, it would mean not just losing face but also turning his back on what he sees as Russia's historic birthright. It is worth remembering that under the presidency of Dmitry Medvedev, Moscow never embraced the prospect of a so-called reset of U.S.-Russian relations; it simply regarded Washington's conciliatory pose as a long-overdue adjustment. The impulse to avenge past geopolitical humiliations has intensified in Putin's current presidential term. And now, the crisis in Ukraine has elevated its champions. For the country's hodgepodge of hard-liners and nationalists, Utkin said, "confrontation is a plus," in that it "allows the acquisition of ever more sovereignty."

Further confrontation with the West over Ukraine may look attractive to Putin, who drew a clear lesson from the denouement of the Cold War: to yield is to risk collapse. Faced with scrapping or intensifying his Ukraine adventure after the shooting down of MH17, Putin chose the latter course, even at the cost of global opprobrium. Russia is now preparing to hunker down for a prolonged period of isolation from the West, referred to in Moscow's political circles as "mobilization," "consolidation," or "self-sufficiency."

In practice, this will mean fetishizing Russia's exclusion from such bodies as the G-8 while expanding efforts to replace foreign products and services with homegrown ones. On Wednesday, Putin announced a ban on food products from countries that have enacted sanctions against Russia—a move that may hurt Russian consumers more than U.S. or European producers, given that imports make up about 30 percent of the retail food market. (Other proposals under discussion range from the probable, such as insourcing parts for the arms industry, to the problematic, such as building a national credit card payment system.) Russia will turn inward, tightening its domestic politics while embracing confrontation abroad. Changing Putin's calculus, to the extent such a thing is even possible, could take years. "Sanctions aren't a pill you swallow today that is going to work tomorrow," said a U.S. official familiar with Ukraine, adding that the Obama administration hopes the long-term dangers for Putin affect his thinking today.

Putin has wagered his presidency on the idea that he can weather the costs of isolation without stoking the sort of social unrest that would challenge his authority. He may be right. Writing in the respected business daily *Vedomosti* last week, Vasily Kashin, a political analyst sympathetic to the Kremlin, described how "in the first years of this new cold war, we will heroically overcome difficulties, and then we will achieve victory, for which our grandchildren will have to foot the bill."

In the short run, the very things that have harmed Russia economically may now protect Putin politically. In June, Clifford Gaddy and Barry Ickes of the Brookings Institution described Russia as "the cockroach of economies—primitive and inelegant in many respects but possessing a remarkable ability to survive in the most adverse and varying conditions." U.S. and EU sanctions will likely cause Russia's GDP growth rate, which was already declining before the Ukraine crisis, to fall even more precipitously. But the latest sanctions do not block Russia's oil and gas exports, which account for around half of the Kremlin's budget. Those revenues will continue to flow into state coffers and from there into the pockets of the large contingent of Russians whose livelihoods depend on the government. (About 20 percent of Russians are pensioners, 20 percent work for the state, and 15 percent work for state-owned companies.) And so the sanctions will put little pressure on wages, which are central to political stability. As Vladislav Inozemtsev, an economist and the director of the Centre for Post-Industrial Studies, put it, "Sanctions will take a hit on growth, but they can't keep Putin from raising salaries of bureaucrats and FSB officers."

At the same time, although economic isolation may aggrieve many inside the business elite, they will not necessarily find this reason enough to turn against Putin. As foreign banks stop lending, Russian firms will be forced to turn to the state for fresh financing and the cash to pay back debts. The larger Russian banks will need to refinance around $50 billion in debt by the end of next year; Russian firms have around $100 billion to pay down. Moscow's businesspeople may resent Putin, but they will be more bound to him than ever. And as the state reinforces its primacy as the economy's largest investor, it will put capital toward large, unwieldy projects, such as heavy industry or infrastructure construction. Putin's most natural supporters stand to benefit. Their influence will grow at the expense of those whose livelihoods are tied to the global economy.

Russia may be able to insulate itself with hydrocarbon revenues at first, but several dangers will reveal themselves before long. The latest sanctions prohibit the transfer of high-tech equipment needed for the exploration of hard-to-reach oil fields in the Arctic and offshore. With the decline of Russia's Siberian fields, which represent 80 percent of current production, the country needs to develop new oil sources. The Russian government has reserve funds in excess of $170 billion, but much of the money it will soon spend must go to propping up the ruble and bailing out state banks and companies. Thus, with private investment already near zero, Russia's last remaining investor—the state itself—will be forced to spend less on investing in the economy and more on damage control.

At that point (perhaps even sooner), a cycle of sinking growth, if not outright recession, is all but guaranteed. The first to suffer will be regional budgets, which are financed by taxes and not energy profits. To fill the looming gap in social spending and salaries in the regions, Putin has floated the idea of introducing a three percent sales tax. Inozemtsev suggested that within two or three years, Russia could see a GDP drop of five percent and significantly higher taxes. Yet, that's practically an eternity in the mentality of Russia's political class. "Our leaders think September is so far away, you could think about it sometime later," he said.

Moreover, any hardship that does appear will be blamed on the machinations of the West. Seeing as 90 percent of Russians get their information primarily from television, the most controlled of all media, Putin may be able to count on this narrative winning out. For a while, at least, a sense of shared mission against an external enemy should compensate for whatever discontent arises. "Society will be ready to forgive Putin for a decrease in living standards," predicted a legislator from the pro-Kremlin political party United Russia. "What does success for a society mean, anyway?" he asked. "Quality of life? Or a historical role for the country, and citizens who feel connected, part of one large, collective unconscious?" The legislator acknowledged that the Kremlin will continue to control politics tightly, leaving little room to maneuver for the country's small number of liberals. The system will become blunter. "I don't like it, but I admit it may be necessary," the legislator said.

As Lev Gudkov, the director of the Levada Center, an independent polling agency, put it, Putin—first through the annexation of Crimea, now through the proxy war in eastern Ukraine—has managed to "colonize the diffuse sense of aggression" that had built up inside Russia over the years, itself the result of a lack of any "basis for positive self-affirmation." But the euphoria has come at little cost. Returning Crimea to Russia was a benevolent gesture, the kind of trophy the tsar delivered to his subjects for free. Putin may enjoy an approval rating above 80 percent, but Russians regularly tell pollsters they think of the state as a distant, corrupt machine. That makes their enthusiasm potentially hollow, Gudkov said. A feeling of helplessness toward the state breeds what he called a sense of "irresponsibility," whereby Russians "don't want to suffer" for Putin's adventurism in Ukraine, however much they appreciate it now.

Much will depend on what happens next in Ukraine. The Ukrainian military surrounds the rebel stronghold of Donetsk and may have managed to cut it off from supplies coming across the Russian border. If pro-Kiev forces wage siege to Donetsk, Putin might feel compelled to act for two reasons: the images of bloodshed among a population Putin claims to be protecting could be impossible to explain away, and the prospect of a battlefield defeat for the rebels would rob Putin of what he sees as his most powerful instrument in determining a future Ukrainian state to his liking. At the moment, Russian troops are engaged in live-fire exercises along the border, complete with 100 military aircraft. These could well presage an invasion under the pretext of a humanitarian operation. Yet Putin's ultimate preference, if he thinks it still tenable, is to wait out Kiev and the West and support the rebels as a viable force for another several months. Over time, the Kremlin hopes, Ukrainian losses will mount, the country's economy will suffer, and the possibility of a winter without Russian gas will sink in. "No one wants to put forces in Ukraine," said Igor Korotchenko, the editor of *National Defense* magazine and a member of the public council of the Russian Ministry of Defense. "Who wants that hemorrhoid?"

The United States and Europe made their own bet with sanctions: that economic isolation will deter Putin from further meddling in Ukraine. And Putin could well prove them right. Although he has given voice to a revanchist ideology of late, he also knows how to play the role of pragmatic tactician. Yet, it is equally possible that he thinks he has less than ever to lose in defending his country's interests, however differently he and Obama may define them. After the MH17 crash and the new sanctions, Korotchenko said, "the circumstances may have changed, but Russia's strategic interests did not." The only thing that may be different, he added, is that "now Putin can make decisions without worrying too much about the consequences—his hands are untied."

China's Imperial President

Xi Jinping Tightens His Grip

Elizabeth C. Economy

FROM OUR NOVEMBER/ DECEMBER 2014 ISSUE

Chinese President Xi Jinping has articulated a simple but powerful vision: the rejuvenation of the Chinese nation. It is a patriotic call to arms, drawing inspiration from the glories of China's imperial past and the ideals of its socialist present to promote political unity at home and influence abroad. After just two years in office, Xi has advanced himself as a transformative leader, adopting an agenda that proposes to reform, if not revolutionize, political and economic relations not only within China but also with the rest of the world.

Underlying Xi's vision is a growing sense of urgency. Xi assumed power at a moment when China, despite its economic success, was politically adrift. The Chinese Communist Party, plagued by corruption and lacking a compelling ideology, had lost credibility among the public, and social unrest was on the rise. The Chinese economy, still growing at an impressive clip, had begun to show signs of strain and uncertainty. And on the international front, despite its position as a global economic power, China was punching well below its weight. Beijing had failed to respond effectively to the crises in Libya and Syria and had stood by as political change rocked two of its closest partners, Myanmar (also known

ELIZABETH C. ECONOMY is C. V. Starr Senior Fellow and Director for Asia Studies at the Council on Foreign Relations.

as Burma) and North Korea. To many observers, it appeared as though China had no overarching foreign policy strategy.

Xi has reacted to this sense of malaise with a power grab—for himself, for the Communist Party, and for China. He has rejected the communist tradition of collective leadership, instead establishing himself as the paramount leader within a tightly centralized political system. At home, his proposed economic reforms will bolster the role of the market but nonetheless allow the state to retain significant control. Abroad, Xi has sought to elevate China by expanding trade and investment, creating new international institutions, and strengthening the military. His vision contains an implicit fear: that an open door to Western political and economic ideas will undermine the power of the Chinese state.

If successful, Xi's reforms could yield a corruption-free, politically cohesive, and economically powerful one-party state with global reach: a Singapore on steroids. But there is no guarantee that the reforms will be as transformative as Xi hopes. His policies have created deep pockets of domestic discontent and provoked an international backlash. To silence dissent, Xi has launched a political crackdown, alienating many of the talented and resourceful Chinese citizens his reforms are intended to encourage. His tentative economic steps have raised questions about the country's prospects for continued growth. And his winner-take-all mentality has undermined his efforts to become a global leader.

The United States and the rest of the world cannot afford to wait and see how his reforms play out. The United States should be ready to embrace some of Xi's initiatives as opportunities for international collaboration while treating others as worrisome trends that must be stopped before they are solidified.

A DOMESTIC CRACKDOWN

Xi's vision for a rejuvenated China rests above all on his ability to realize his particular brand of political reform: consolidating personal power by creating new institutions, silencing political opposition, and legitimizing his leadership and the Communist Party's power in the eyes of the Chinese people. Since taking office, Xi has moved quickly to amass political power and to become, within the Chinese leadership, not first among equals but simply first. He serves as head of the Communist Party and the Central Military Commission, the two traditional pillars of Chinese party leadership, as well as the head of leading groups on the economy, military reform, cybersecurity, Taiwan, and foreign affairs and a commission on national security. Unlike previous presidents, who have let their premiers act as the state's authority on the economy, Xi has assumed that role for himself. He has also taken a highly personal command of the Chinese military: this past spring, he received public proclamations of allegiance from 53 senior military officials. According to one former general, such pledges have been made only three times previously in Chinese history.

In his bid to consolidate power, Xi has also sought to eliminate alternative political voices, particularly on China's once lively Internet. The government has detained, arrested, or publicly humiliated popular bloggers such as the billionaire businessmen Pan Shiyi and Charles Xue. Such commentators, with tens of millions of followers on social media, used to routinely discuss issues ranging from environmental pollution to censorship to child trafficking. Although they have not been completely silenced, they no longer stray into sensitive political territory. Indeed, Pan, a central figure in the campaign to force the Chinese government to improve Beijing's air quality, was compelled to criticize himself on national television in 2013. Afterward, he took to Weibo, a popular Chinese microblogging service, to warn a fellow real estate billionaire against criticizing the government's program of economic reform: "Careful, or you might be arrested."

Under Xi, Beijing has also issued a raft of new Internet regulations. One law threatens punishment of up to three years in prison for posting anything that the authorities consider to be a "rumor," if the post is either read by more than 5,000 people or forwarded over 500 times. Under these stringent new laws, Chinese citizens have been arrested for posting theories about the disappearance of

Malaysia Airlines Flight 370. Over one four-month period, Beijing suspended, deleted, or sanctioned more than 100,000 accounts on Weibo for violating one of the seven broadly defined "bottom lines" that represent the limits of permissible expression. These restrictions produced a 70 percent drop in posts on Weibo from March 2012 to December 2013, according to a study of 1.6 million Weibo users commissioned by The Telegraph. And when Chinese netizens found alternative ways of communicating, for example, by using the group instant-messaging platform WeChat, government censors followed them. In August 2014, Beijing issued new instant-messaging regulations that required users to register with their real names, restricted the sharing of political news, and enforced a code of conduct. Unsurprisingly, in its 2013 ranking of Internet freedom around the world, the U.S.-based nonprofit Freedom House ranked China 58 out of 60 countries—tied with Cuba. Only Iran ranked lower.

In his efforts to promote ideological unity, Xi has also labeled ideas from abroad that challenge China's political system as unpatriotic and even dangerous. Along these lines, Beijing has banned academic research and teaching on seven topics: universal values, civil society, citizens' rights, freedom of the press, mistakes made by the Communist Party, the privileges of capitalism, and the independence of the judiciary. This past summer, a party official publicly attacked the Chinese Academy of Social Sciences, a government research institution, for having been "infiltrated by foreign forces." This attack was met with mockery among prominent Chinese intellectuals outside the academy, including the economist Mao Yushi, the law professor He Weifang, and the writer Liu Yiming. Still, the accusations will likely have a chilling effect on scholarly research and international collaboration.

This crackdown might undermine the very political cohesiveness Xi seeks. Residents of Hong Kong and Macao, who have traditionally enjoyed more political freedom than those on the mainland, have watched Xi's moves with growing unease; many have called for democratic reform. In raucously democratic Taiwan,

Xi's repressive tendencies are unlikely to help promote reunification with the mainland. And in the ethnically divided region of Xinjiang, Beijing's restrictive political and cultural policies have resulted in violent protests.

Even within China's political and economic upper class, many have expressed concern over Xi's political tightening and are seeking a foothold overseas. According to the China-based *Hurun Report*, 85 percent of those with assets of more than $1 million want their children to be educated abroad, and more than 65 percent of Chinese citizens with assets of $1.6 million or more have emigrated or plan to do so. The flight of China's elites has become not only a political embarrassment but also a significant setback for Beijing's efforts to lure back home top scientists and scholars who have moved abroad in past decades.

A MORAL AUTHORITY?

The centerpiece of Xi's political reforms is his effort to restore the moral authority of the Communist Party. He has argued that failing to address the party's endemic corruption could lead to the demise of not only the party but also the Chinese state. Under the close supervision of Wang Qishan, a member of the Politburo Standing Committee, tackling official corruption has become Xi's signature issue. Previous Chinese leaders have carried out anticorruption campaigns, but Xi has brought new energy and seriousness to the cause: limiting funds for official banquets, cars, and meals; pursuing well-known figures in the media, the government, the military, and the private sector; and dramatically increasing the number of corruption cases brought for official review. In 2013, the party punished more than 182,000 officials for corruption, 50,000 more than the annual average for the previous five years. Two scandals that broke this past spring indicate the scale of the campaign. In the first, federal authorities arrested a lieutenant general in the Chinese military for selling hundreds of positions in the armed forces, sometimes for extraordinary sums; the price to become a major general, for example, reached $4.8 million. In the second,

Beijing began investigating more than 500 members of the regional government in Hunan Province for participating in an $18 million vote-buying ring.

Xi's anticorruption crusade represents just one part of his larger plan to reclaim the Communist Party's moral authority. He has also announced reforms that address some of Chinese society's most pressing concerns. With Xi at the helm, the Chinese leadership has launched a campaign to improve the country's air quality; reformed the one-child policy; revised the *hukou* system of residency permits, which ties a citizen's housing, health care, and education to his official residence and tends to favor urban over rural residents; and shut down the system of "reeducation through labor" camps, which allowed the government to detain people without cause. The government has also announced plans to make the legal system more transparent and to rid it of meddling by local officials.

Despite the impressive pace and scope of Xi's reform initiatives, it remains unclear whether they represent the beginning of longer-term change, or if they are merely superficial measures designed to buy the short-term goodwill of the people. Either way, some of his reforms have provoked fierce opposition. According to the *Financial Times*, former Chinese leaders Jiang Zemin and Hu Jintao have both warned Xi to rein in his anticorruption campaign, and Xi himself has conceded that his efforts have met with significant resistance. The campaign has also incurred real economic costs. According to a report by Bank of America Merrill Lynch, Chinese GDP could fall this year by as much as 1.5 percentage points as a result of declining sales of luxury goods and services, as officials are increasingly concerned that lavish parties, political favor-buying, and expensive purchases will invite unwanted attention. (Of course, many Chinese are still buying; they are just doing so abroad.) And even those who support the goal of fighting corruption have questioned Xi's methods. Premier Li Keqiang, for example, called for greater transparency and public accountability in the government's anticorruption campaign in early 2014; his remarks, however, were quickly deleted from websites.

Xi's stance on corruption may also pose a risk to his personal and political standing: his family ranks among the wealthiest of the Chinese leadership, and according to *The New York Times*, Xi has told relatives to shed their assets, reducing his vulnerability to attack. Moreover, he has resisted calls for greater transparency, arresting activists who have pushed for officials to reveal their assets and punishing Western media outlets that have investigated Chinese leaders.

KEEPING CONTROL

As Xi strives to consolidate political control and restore the Communist Party's legitimacy, he must also find ways to stir more growth in China's economy. Broadly speaking, his objectives include transforming China from the world's manufacturing center to its innovation hub, rebalancing the Chinese economy by prioritizing consumption over investment, and expanding the space for private enterprise. Xi's plans include both institutional and policy reforms. He has slated the tax system, for example, for a significant overhaul: local revenues will come from a broad range of taxes instead of primarily from land sales, which led to corruption and social unrest. In addition, the central government, which traditionally has received roughly half the national tax revenue while paying for just one-third of the expenditures for social welfare, will increase the funding it provides for social services, relieving some of the burden on local governments. Scores of additional policy initiatives are also in trial phases, including encouraging private investment in state-owned enterprises and lowering the compensation of their executives, establishing private banks to direct capital to small and medium-sized businesses, and shortening the length of time it takes for new businesses to secure administrative approvals.

Yet as details of Xi's economic plan unfold, it has become clear that despite his emphasis on the free market, the state will retain control over much of the economy. Reforming the way in which state-owned enterprises are governed will not undermine the dominant role of the Communist Party in these companies' decision-making; Xi has kept in place significant barriers to foreign investment; and even as the government pledges a shift away from investment-led growth, its stimulus efforts continue, contributing to growing levels of local debt. Indeed, according to the Global Times, a Chinese newspaper, the increase in the value of outstanding nonperforming loans in the first six months of 2014 exceeded the value of new nonperforming loans for all of 2013.

Moreover, Xi has infused his economic agenda with the same nationalist—even xenophobic—sentiment that permeates his political agenda. His aggressive anticorruption and antimonopoly campaigns have targeted multinational corporations making products that include powdered milk, medical supplies, pharmaceuticals, and auto parts. In July 2013, in fact, China's National Development and Reform Commission brought together representatives from 30 multinational companies in an attempt to force them to admit to wrongdoing. At times, Beijing appears to be deliberately undermining foreign goods and service providers: the state-controlled media pay a great deal of attention to alleged wrongdoing at multinational companies while remaining relatively quiet about similar problems at Chinese firms.

Like his anticorruption campaign, Xi's investigation of foreign companies raises questions about the underlying intent. In a widely publicized debate broadcast by Chinese state television between the head of the European Union Chamber of Commerce in China and an official from the National Development and Reform Commission, the European official forced his Chinese counterpart to defend the seeming disparities between the Chinese government's treatment of foreign and domestic companies. Eventually, the Chinese official appeared to yield, saying that China's antimonopoly procedure was a procedure "with Chinese characteristics."

The early promise of Xi's overhaul thus remains unrealized. A 31-page scorecard of Chinese economic reform, published in June 2014 by the U.S.-China Business Council, contains dozens of unfulfilled mandates. It deems just three of Xi's policy initiatives successes: reducing the time it takes to register new businesses, allowing multinational corporations to use Chinese currency to expand their business, and reforming the *hukou* system. Tackling deeper reforms, however, may require a jolt to the system, such as the collapse of the housing market. For now, Xi may well be his own worst enemy: calls for market dominance are no match for his desire to retain economic control.

WAKING THE LION

Xi's efforts to transform politics and economics at home have been matched by equally dramatic moves to establish China as a global power. The roots of Xi's foreign policy, however, predate his presidency. The Chinese leadership began publicly discussing China's rise as a world power in the wake of the 2008 global financial crisis, when many Chinese analysts argued that the United States had begun an inevitable decline that would leave room for China at the top of the global pecking order. In a speech in Paris in March 2014, Xi recalled Napoleon's ruminations on China: "Napoleon said that China is a sleeping lion, and when she wakes, the world will shake." The Chinese lion, Xi assured his audience, "has already awakened, but this is a peaceful, pleasant, and civilized lion." Yet some of Xi's actions belie his comforting words. He has replaced the decades-old mantra of the former Chinese leader Deng Xiaoping—"Hide brightness, cherish obscurity"—with a far more expansive and muscular foreign policy.

For Xi, all roads lead to Beijing, figuratively and literally. He has revived the ancient concept of the Silk Road—which connected the Chinese empire to Central Asia, the Middle East, and even Europe—by proposing a vast network of railroads, pipelines, highways, and canals to follow the contours of the old route. The infrastructure, which Xi expects Chinese banks and companies to finance and build, would allow for more trade between China and much of the rest of the world. Beijing has also considered building a roughly 8,100-mile high-speed intercontinental railroad that would connect China to Canada, Russia, and the United States through the Bering Strait. Even the Arctic has become China's backyard: Chinese scholars describe their country as a "near-Arctic" state.

Along with new infrastructure, Xi also wants to establish new institutions to support China's position as a regional and global leader. He has helped create a new development bank, operated by the BRICS countries—Brazil, Russia, India, China, and South Africa—to challenge the primacy of the International Monetary Fund and the World Bank. And he has advanced the establishment of the Asian Infrastructure Investment Bank, which could enable China to become the leading financer of regional development. These two efforts signal Xi's desire to capitalize on frustrations with the United States' unwillingness to make international economic organizations more representative of developing countries.

Xi has also promoted new regional security initiatives. In addition to the already existing Shanghai Cooperation Organization, a Chinese-led security institution that includes Russia and four Central Asian states, Xi wants to build a new Asia-Pacific security structure that would exclude the United States. Speaking at a conference in May 2014, Xi underscored the point: "It is for the people of Asia to run the affairs of Asia, solve the problems of Asia, and uphold the security of Asia."

Xi's predilection for a muscular regional policy became evident well before his presidency. In 2010, Xi chaired the leading group responsible for the country's South China Sea policy, which broadened its definition of China's core interests to include its expansive claims to maritime territory in the South China Sea. Since then, he has used everything from the Chinese navy to fishing boats to try to secure these claims—claims disputed by other nations bordering the sea. In May 2014, conflict between China and Vietnam erupted when the China National Petroleum Corporation moved an oil rig into a disputed area in the South China Sea; tensions remained high until China withdrew the rig in mid-July. To help enforce China's claims to the East China Sea, Xi has declared an "air defense identification zone" over part of it, overlapping with those established by Japan and South Korea. He has also announced regional fishing regulations. None of China's neighbors has recognized any of these steps as legitimate. But Beijing has even redrawn the map of China embossed on Chinese passports to incorporate areas under dispute with India, as well as with countries in Southeast Asia, provoking a political firestorm.

These maneuvers have stoked nationalist sentiments at home and equally virulent nationalism abroad. New, similarly nationalist leaders in India and Japan have expressed concern over Xi's policies and taken measures to raise their countries' own security profiles. Indeed, during his campaign for the Indian prime ministership in early 2014, Narendra Modi criticized China's expansionist tendencies, and he and Japanese Prime Minister Shinzo Abe have since upgraded their countries' defense and security ties. Several new regional security efforts are under way that exclude Beijing (as well as Washington). For example, India has been training some Southeast Asian navies, including those of Myanmar and Vietnam, and many of the region's militaries—including those of Australia, India, Japan, the Philippines, Singapore, and South Korea—have planned joint defense exercises.

A VIGOROUS RESPONSE

For the United States and much of the rest of the world, the awakening of Xi's China provokes two different reactions: excitement, on the one hand, about what a stronger, less corrupt China could achieve, and significant concern, on the other hand, over the challenges an authoritarian, militaristic China might pose to the U.S.-backed liberal order.

On the plus side, Beijing's plans for a new Silk Road hinge on political stability in the Middle East; that might provide Beijing with an incentive to work with Washington to secure peace in the region. Similarly, Chinese companies' growing interest in investing abroad might give Washington greater leverage as it pushes forward a bilateral investment treaty with Beijing. The United States should also encourage China's participation in the Trans-Pacific Partnership, a major regional free-trade agreement under negotiation. Just as China's negotiations to join the World Trade Organization in the 1990s prompted Chinese economic reformers to advance change at home, negotiations to join the TPP might do the same today.

In addition, although China already has a significant stake in the international system, the United States must work to keep China in the fold. For example, the U.S. Congress should ratify proposed changes to the International Monetary Fund's internal voting system that would grant China and other developing countries a larger say in the fund's management and thereby reduce Beijing's determination to establish competing groups.

On the minus side, Xi's nationalist rhetoric and assertive military posture pose a direct challenge to U.S. interests in the region and call for a vigorous response. Washington's "rebalance," or "pivot," to Asia represents more than simply a response to China's more assertive behavior. It also reflects the United States' most closely held foreign policy values: freedom of the seas, the air, and space; free trade; the rule of law; and basic human rights. Without a strong pivot, the United States' role as a regional power will diminish, and Washington will be denied the benefits of deeper engagement with many of the world's most dynamic economies. The United States should therefore back up the pivot with a strong military presence in the Asia-Pacific to deter or counter Chinese aggression; reach consensus and then ratify the TPP; and bolster U.S. programs that support democratic institutions and civil society in such places as Cambodia, Malaysia, Myanmar, and Vietnam, where democracy is nascent but growing.

At the same time, Washington should realize that Xi may not be successful in transforming China in precisely the ways he has articulated. He has set out his vision, but pressures from both inside and outside China will shape the country's path forward in unexpected ways. Some commodity-rich countries have balked at dealing with Chinese firms, troubled by the their weak record of social responsibility, which has forced Beijing to explore new ways of doing business. China's neighbors, alarmed by Beijing's swagger, have begun to form new security relationships. Even prominent foreign policy experts within China, such as Peking University's Wang Jisi and the retired ambassador Wu Jianmin, have expressed reservations over the tenor of Xi's foreign policy.

Finally, although little in Xi's domestic or foreign policy appears to welcome deeper engagement with the United States, Washington should resist framing its relationship with China as a competition. Treating China as a competitor or foe merely feeds Xi's anti-Western narrative, undermines those in China pushing for moderation, and does little to advance bilateral cooperation and much to diminish the stature of the United States. Instead, the White House should pay particular attention to the evolution of Xi's policies, taking advantage of those that could strengthen its relationship with China and pushing back against those that undermine U.S. interests. In the face of uncertainty over China's future, U.S. policymakers must remain flexible and fleet-footed.

Keep Hope Alive

How to Prevent U.S.-Chinese Relations From Blowing Up

James B. Steinberg
and Michael O'Hanlon

FROM OUR JULY/
AUGUST 2014 ISSUE

At their summit in California last June, U.S. President Barack Obama and Chinese President Xi Jinping committed themselves to building trust between their countries. Since then, new official forums for communication have been launched (such as the military-to-military dialogues recently announced by the two countries' defense ministers), complementing existing forums such as the Strategic and Economic Dialogue (which features the countries' top diplomats and economic officials). But despite these efforts, trust in both capitals—and in the countries at large—remains scarce, and the possibility of an accidental or even intentional conflict between the United States and China seems to be growing. Given the vast potential costs such a conflict would carry for both sides, figuring out how to keep it at bay is among the most important international challenges of the coming years and decades.

JAMES STEINBERG is Dean of the Maxwell School of Citizenship and Public Affairs and Professor of Social Science, International Affairs, and Law at Syracuse University.

MICHAEL O'HANLON is a Senior Fellow at the Center for 21st Century Security and Intelligence and Director of Research for the Foreign Policy Program at the Brookings Institution. They are the authors of *Strategic Reassurance and Resolve: U.S.-China Relations in the Twenty-first Century* (Princeton University Press, 2014), from which this essay is adapted.

The factors undermining trust are easy to state. East Asia's security and economic landscape is undergoing massive, tectonic change, driven primarily by China's remarkable economic rise in recent decades. That economic miracle, in turn, has made it possible for China to increase its military capacity and ramp up its political role in the region and beyond. China's leaders and prominent strategists have been at pains to insist that China's rise will be peaceful and poses no threat to its neighbors or the existing international political and economic order. But many members of the world community remain concerned and even skeptical, noting that history and international relations theory are replete with examples of conflict arising from clashes between a dominant and a rising power.

Such skepticism has been fueled, moreover, by China's own recent actions, from its assertive maritime operations in the East China and South China seas to its unilateral proclamation of an "air defense identification zone" around the Diaoyu Islands (known in Japan as the Senkaku Islands), in the East China Sea. And U.S. military planners have become increasingly concerned about the trajectory of China's military modernization and about its "anti-access/area-denial" (A2/AD) doctrine, which they see as an ill-disguised effort by China to weaken the United States' ability to defend its interests and support its alliance commitments in the western Pacific.

At the same time, the Obama team has been actively promoting its own strategic reorientation, the "pivot," or "rebalance," to Asia. The administration insists that its motivation is to enhance regional stability for the benefit of all, rather than to contain or threaten China. But few Chinese, particularly in the military and national security communities, are convinced. They, too, read their history and international relations theory and conclude that the United States, like most dominant powers before it, is determined to maintain its hegemonic dominance, thwarting China's rise and keeping it vulnerable. As evidence of malign American intent, they point to enhanced U.S. capabilities, such as expanded regional missile defense; new and augmented basing arrangements in Australia, Guam, and Singapore; and recent military exercises and reconnaissance conducted close to Chinese territory, as well as the persistence of Cold War–era security alliances. And the only plausible justification for the emerging U.S. military concept of "air-sea battle," they claim, is a desire to coerce China with the threat of a decapitating preemptive attack.

Given the uncertainty surrounding the future of Asian security, each side's actions can be understood and legitimized as measures designed to hedge against the possibility of future hostility or aggression on the part of the other. But it is just such rational short-term thinking that can generate a longer-term spiral into even greater mistrust, making future conflict a self-fulfilling prophecy—which is why it is crucial to find ways of transcending or minimizing such a classic security dilemma.

One way to head off unnecessary conflicts is to reduce the malign role played by misperceptions. These can emerge from two quite opposite directions: from one side either perceiving a threat where none is intended or failing to believe in the credibility of the other side's intent to defend its interests. This means that the practical challenge for both Washington and Beijing is to dispel false fears while sustaining deterrence by making credible threats where they are seriously intended. The good news is that history and theory suggest four tools can be helpful in this regard: restraint, reciprocity, transparency, and resilience.

Restraint is the willingness to forgo actions that might enhance one's own security but that will appear threatening to somebody else. Reciprocity is a response in kind by one side to the other's actions—in this case, a signal that restraint is being understood as forbearance (rather than weakness) and is being met with emulation rather than exploitation. Transparency helps allay fears that the other side's visible positive gestures mask hidden, more hostile intentions. And resilience provides a margin of safety in keeping crises from escalating and in making it easier for either side to try to start a virtuous cycle of restraint, reciprocity, and transparency.

Fortunately for everybody, there are a variety of practical measures both Washington and Beijing can take in national security policy that can bring these tools to bear in increasing trust and reducing the risk of conflict.

CONVENTIONAL THINKING

From Washington's perspective, the greatest uncertainty about China's future intentions stems from the rapid and sustained growth of Chinese military spending and the accompanying investment in sophisticated conventional armaments that challenge U.S. capabilities. It is true that even the most generous assessments of China's current military spending—that it approaches $200 billion annually, or about two percent of GDP—still put it at less than a third of U.S. spending (currently $600 billion a year, or about 3.5 percent of GDP). At current rates of growth, Beijing's annual military budget would not equal Washington's until around 2030. And even then, the United States could rely on large accumulated stocks of modern weaponry, years of combat experience, and the spending of its allies and partners (now around $400 billion annually).

But if China wants to calm international fears and signal that its goals are legitimate self-defense rather than the ability to project power abroad and threaten others, there are several constructive steps it could take. Given that U.S. spending covers capabilities not just in Asia but around the globe, a convincing case can be made that China can achieve adequate self-defense by spending about half of what the United States does. By reducing the current rate of growth of its military budget in coming years, therefore, China could telegraph that its objective is self-defense rather than complete parity. And it could exercise restraint in acquiring weapon systems (such as long-range antiship ballistic missiles) whose purpose, especially if procured in large numbers, seems inconsistent with a claim that it welcomes the U.S. military presence in the western Pacific. More broadly, China could offer greater transparency about its military budget and spending and provide greater clarity about the goals of its A2/AD doctrine.

The United States, in turn, could take steps to make clear that its own conventional military modernization is not designed to threaten legitimate Chinese security interests. The declining U.S. military budget is one such show of restraint. But Washington could do more in this regard, such as by clarifying the purpose of its air-sea battle concept, changing the concept's name to "air-sea operations," including military services besides the navy and the air force more centrally in U.S. Asia policy, and modifying some of the more "offensive-minded" features of the air-sea doctrine that appear to directly threaten China's command-and-control and strategic assets with a possible preemptive attack early in a conflict. To enhance the credibility of such doctrinal modifications, the United States could cap its procurement of long-range, precision-guided ballistic missiles and strategic bombers, which if acquired in sufficient numbers could be seen as posing an existential threat to China. By deploying a mix of conventional assets that did not require a heavy reliance on early escalation (including bases that were more effectively hardened and assets that were more survivable in the face of an attack), Washington could help mitigate a U.S.-Chinese arms race and lessen the risk of a conflict breaking out early in a crisis.

FROM SPACE TO CYBERSPACE

The most iconic confidence-building measures during the Cold War were strategic arms control agreements, which despite some problems ultimately helped Washington and Moscow increase crisis stability and limit offensive and defensive nuclear arms races. For various reasons, formal arms control agreements are less well suited to contemporary U.S.-Chinese relations than they were to U.S.-Soviet relations and could in some cases prove counterproductive. That said, there are a number of steps in the unconventional weapons arena that could help allay mutual suspicion and reduce the likelihood of accidental or premature escalation of conflict.

Take space, for example. Given the deep U.S. dependence on satellites for both military and civilian purposes, Chinese planners

are clearly considering how to neutralize the advantages space offers for U.S. military operations. Yet precisely because of that dependence, the United States would be under pressure to act
forcefully and quickly if it believed those assets were at risk, leaving little time for fact-finding or diplomacy to defuse a crisis. For
this reason, measures that can enhance the security of Washington's space assets are particularly compelling, and they will become
more attractive to Beijing, too, as it increases its space capability
over time. Absolute security in space cannot be guaranteed, since
every maneuverable civilian satellite has the inherent capacity to
destroy another satellite. But by adopting measures such as agreed-
on "keep-out zones" around satellites, norms of behavior can be
established that legitimate the use of force in self-defense without
having such use be seen as provocative. Resilience is important
here, too, as the United States will need redundancy in space and
aerial systems to compensate for a certain unavoidable degree of
vulnerability.

Similarly, the United States and China could agree to a treaty,
ideally involving other countries as well, banning collisions or ex-
plosions that would produce debris above an altitude of roughly
1,000 miles in space, the zone where low-earth-orbit satellites routinely operate. This area is already becoming cluttered with debris
in ways that could render future space operations dangerous, and
since tests of missile defense systems typically take place at a lower
altitude, such an arrangement would be all gain with little pain.
The two sides could also agree not to develop or test dedicated
antisatellite weapons or space-to-ground weapons. Testing constraints alone would not eliminate the potential for such capabilities, of course, but they could reduce the confidence each side had
in them, along with the willingness to invest in and rely on what
would be rendered potentially destabilizing systems of uncertain
effectiveness.

Restraint can play a particularly important role in enhancing
confidence in the nuclear realm. China's restraint thus far in its
nuclear deployments, for example, helps give credibility to the

defensive nature of its nuclear doctrine. Similarly, U.S. restraint in deploying large numbers of ballistic missile interceptors that could neutralize China's retaliatory capability offers reassurance of American defensive intent. Even without formal codification, continued observance of this restraint would build trust, which could be further strengthened by both sides' ratification of the Comprehensive Nuclear Test Ban Treaty and implementation of the verification regime that accompanies it.

Such measures could be enhanced by transparency agreements, such as an "open skies" regime, which would give further credibility to each side's restraint. This regime could build on the arrangement by which the United States and Russia, and other NATO and former Warsaw Pact states, conduct overflights of each other's territories (at the rate of roughly 100 flights a year) under an accord dating from the early 1990s. Countries know how to protect their most precious secrets from such overflights, so the arrangement presents no true national security concerns. But such an accord could lessen Beijing's frustration over routine U.S. reconnaissance flights near Chinese coastlines. Such flights could even be modestly reduced, as former National Security Adviser Zbigniew Brzezinski has proposed—a step that merits serious study, particularly if China shows a willingness to reciprocate with greater transparency.

Cyberspace is especially challenging. As in space, the United States' high degree of dependence on its cyber-infrastructure poses vulnerabilities and creates pressure to respond quickly to any attack, possibly even before its source can be fully identified. And the recent U.S. focus on "active defense" of this infrastructure seems to imply Washington's willingness to act offensively to neutralize emerging threats, with all the attendant danger of escalating retaliation.

There are many reasons to believe that both Washington and Beijing are unlikely to target cyber-infrastructure unless and until they find themselves on the brink of a major conflict. If nothing else, the countries' mutual economic dependence offers protection against a surprise attack. But other parties, including nonstate actors such as terrorists or hackers, might have an interest in faking such an attack in order to trigger a crisis or even war. For that reason, the United States and China should agree to joint investigation of "anonymous" cyberattacks, establishing transparency and a credible commitment to avoid targeting each other's civilian infrastructure. And resilience is particularly important in cyberspace, since the more each side reduces its vulnerability to a "bolt from the blue" attack, the more time will be available to try to figure out what actually happened and reduce the risk of an unintended spiral of escalation.

NEIGHBORHOOD WATCH

The most likely prospect for a direct military encounter between the United States and China in the near term comes from the growing tensions in the East China and South China seas. U.S. security commitments to Japan and the Philippines, both of which have territorial disputes with China, and U.S. willingness to assert basic navigational rights in the region (which set the stage for a close encounter between the USS *Cowpens* and Chinese ships last December) could entangle Washington in a conflict even though the United States itself has no territorial claims in the area. These tensions are not likely to be resolved anytime soon. The actual interests at stake are small, and many of the conflicts involved could be managed were there sufficient mutual will to do so. But all involved seem to fear that any show of restraint or accommodation will be taken as a sign of weakness, leading to even more assertive behavior in the future. This makes it all the more important to find ways of preventing crises from emerging or keeping them contained once they do so.

China could provide reassurance about its intentions by agreeing to and implementing the Association of Southeast Asian Nations' proposed code of conduct for the South China Sea. Restraining its military deployments and agreeing to operational procedures that would reduce the danger of accidents or miscalculations would make Beijing's assertions of peaceful intent more credible, and similar procedures could be agreed on in connection with the Diaoyu/Senkaku Islands. (This is an area where the bigger policy change needs to come from Beijing; there are other areas where a disproportionate burden of the responsibility lies with Washington, such as in a reduction in the size of offensive nuclear forces in coordination with Russia.)

U.S. and Chinese officials, moreover, need to establish better mechanisms for clear and direct communication during a crisis. Since 1998, the two countries have had a hot line connecting their political leaderships, but they have little military-to-military communication, due largely to Beijing's wariness of such engagement. A military maritime agreement, also dating to 1998, encourages consultation and transparency on each country's respective activities but doesn't cover operational rules of the road or specific tactical movements. It would make sense to establish a formal military hot line patterned after the U.S.-Soviet one; at a minimum, the two countries should each possess a much more complete set of contacts for the other's top military leaders to facilitate rapid communication in crisis situations.

The two sides, and perhaps other regional actors, could also agree to an incidents-at-sea accord comparable to that between Washington and Moscow during the Cold War, including not only navies but also coast guards and perhaps even merchant vessels as well. Both sides will inevitably and legitimately continue their surveillance, but they could do so with far less risk. The accord would be designed to ensure that ships do not approach one another too closely, that carrier air operations are not interfered with, and that submarines do not surface or behave in other potentially risky ways.

Regarding regional issues, even though another Korean war seems unlikely, events on the peninsula in recent years (such as North Korea's ongoing nuclear and missile programs and its sinking of the South Korean frigate *Cheonan* and shelling of Yeonpyeong Island in 2010) serve as reminders that the risk of escalation to a wider conflict persists. Should a crisis erupt as a result of new provocations or a North Korean collapse, it is not hard to imagine the United States and China being drawn in, with potentially tragic consequences. So taking practical steps now to lay the groundwork for a coordinated response to a possible future crisis makes sense.

At the least, each side could reassure the other that its crisis response plans (including to secure North Korean nuclear materials or restore political order) are designed to be stabilizing rather than threatening. For Beijing, the reluctance to talk about such subjects for fear of offending Pyongyang could be circumvented by beginning the conversation as a track-two discussion among academics and retired officials. Beijing should also recognize that on a reunified peninsula, Seoul would have the decision over whether American forces should stay. Washington, for its part, should assure Beijing that any future U.S. force posture on the peninsula (assuming that Seoul would still want some U.S. presence) would be smaller than the current one and not based any further north than it is now. And both Seoul and Washington should be prepared to invite China to help in any future contingency, at least in the northern sectors of North Korea.

Even though cross-strait tensions have eased in recent years, Taiwan remains a contentious issue in U.S.-Chinese relations, in part because China has not renounced the use of force to reunify Taiwan with the mainland and in part because the United States continues to sell arms to Taipei. Some tension would seem to be inevitable given the fundamental differences in interests between the parties. Yet even here, reassurance can play a role. For Beijing, this means making its stated intention of seeking a peaceful path to unification credible, by putting some limits on its military modernization and stopping military exercises focused on intimidating Taiwan through missile barrages or blockades. For Washington, it means making sure that the arms it sells Taipei are in fact defensive and demonstrating a willingness to scale back such arms sales in response to meaningful, observable, and hard-to-reverse reductions in China's threatening stance toward Taiwan.

Fortunately, both sides are already pursuing key elements of such an agenda. However, Beijing's current missile buildup, and the possibility of Washington's countering it by helping Taiwan improve its missile defenses, creates the potential for a new round of escalation—or it could lead to a new round of reassurance. China could usefully start the latter process by reducing its deployed missile force.

MORE SIGNALS, LESS NOISE

The key to stable U.S.-Chinese relations over the long term is for each side to be clear about its true redlines and the price, at least in general terms, it is willing to pay to defend them. As with reassurance, accurately communicating resolve requires more than just words; it involves demonstrating both the will and the capacity to make good on threats.

That means Washington needs to make Beijing understand that it will defend not just its own territory and people but also those of its formal allies and sometimes even its nonallied friends. This is partly what the Obama administration's rebalance was supposed to do, but to achieve that effect, it needs to be followed up on and be executed seriously rather than be allowed to languish. Of course, demonstrating resolve does not have to mean meeting every provocation with a direct military response. Sometimes, nonmilitary responses, such as sanctions and new basing arrangements, may make the most sense, as may using negotiations to offer appropriate "off-ramps" and other avenues for de-escalation of a crisis. The best way to signal resolve prudently in a particular case will depend on various factors, including the degree of coordination Washington can manage to achieve with its allies and partners. But it is crucial to signal to Beijing early and clearly that there are some lines it will not be permitted to cross with impunity.

The flip side of this is that the United States needs to understand and respect China's determination to defend, with force if necessary, its own vital national interests. To the extent that those interests are defined appropriately, this would be an acceptable assertion of China's legitimate right of self-defense under Article 51 of the UN Charter, and given its history of past vulnerability to invasion and aggression, it is understandable for China to take steps to make its own resolve credible. The difficulty here is that in recent years, Beijing has seemed to assert an ever-expanding list of "core" interests and has often handled them truculently, turning even relatively minor and routine disputes into potentially dangerous confrontations and needlessly risky tests of mutual resolve. Beijing needs to recognize that over time, such behavior dilutes the legitimacy and force of its more important claims, sending conflicting signals and undermining its own long-term interests.

U.S.-Chinese relations may be approaching an inflection point. A long-standing bipartisan U.S. consensus on seeking constructive relations with China has frayed, and the Chinese are increasingly pessimistic about the future of bilateral dealings as well. Yet U.S. fatalism about China's rise could lead to resigned acceptance of a new reality or muscular resistance designed to protect old prerogatives—both unpromising and ultimately self-defeating strategies. Building a relationship around the principles of strategic reassurance and resolve offers the prospect of a more promising future without jeopardizing legitimate interests on either side. In effect, rather than simply hoping or planning for trust, it substitutes a "trust but verify" approach. This is much sounder than classic hedging, since it seeks to reduce the possibility of unintended provocation and escalation. And with luck, it can be enough to help keep full-scale conflict at bay, an outcome that prudent people on both sides should be seeking.

Asia for the Asians

Why Chinese-Russian Friendship Is Here to Stay

Gilbert Rozman   OCTOBER 29, 2014

Recently, China and Russia have challenged the international order by giving each other diplomatic backing to confront Ukraine and Hong Kong, respectively. But Western observers have mostly misunderstood the countries' reasons for building closer ties with each other. They have been motivated less by shared material interests than by a common sense of national identity that defines itself in opposition to the West and in support of how each views the legacy of traditional communism. Moscow and Beijing have disagreements about the future order they envision for their regions. But they agree that the geopolitical order of the East should be in opposition to that of the West—and that has led to significantly closer bilateral relations.

Some Western observers have placed an excessive emphasis on Sino-Soviet tensions during the Cold War era, also arguing that the relationship between Beijing and Moscow is likely to remain fragile because of developments in both countries since the 1990s, including democratization in Russia, globalization in China, and the rapid rise of a middle class with access to outside information in both countries. To the extent that China and Russia built ties, these observers believed that the relationship would be a marriage

GILBERT ROZMAN is an Associate Faculty member in the East Asian Studies department at Princeton University. His most recent book is *The Sino-Russian Challenge to the World Order.*

of convenience that would be trumped by other national interests, including good relations with the West.

But most Westerners have failed to understand that, since the 1990s, officials in China and Russia have deeply regretted the Cold War tensions between their countries. They understand that the problem was less a lack of overlap in national interest than national identities skewed by ideological claims to leadership. Moscow made a critical mistake in expecting that Beijing would acquiesce to its leadership, accepting a role as a junior partner. China's leadership did not accept that role, given its obsession with ideological superiority.

Current policymakers in both countries are determined not to repeat these problems. Although China is now in the position to act as the dominant partner in the relationship, it has shown restraint. Leaders in Moscow and Beijing want to avoid allowing chauvinistic nationalism in either country to trump their mutual national interest in minimizing the influence of the West in their respective regions.

To that end, the governments of both countries have been consciously emphasizing foreign policies that dismiss Western legitimacy, while carefully refraining from commenting on the foreign policy ambitions of each other. Chinese President Xi Jinping has described a so-called China Dream that involves a new geopolitical order in Asia built by the governments of that region—with Beijing playing an outsize role. Russian President Vladimir Putin has likewise clarified that his goal is to create a Eurasian Union, in which relations between former Soviet states are determined by Moscow. Both states have accused the United States of following an aggressive Cold War mentality by trying to contain their rightful ambitions in their regions.

There are at least six reasons to believe that this tacit partnership between Russia and China is durable. First, Putin and Xi have been relying on very similar ideologies to justify their rule. They both emphasize pride in the socialist era, Sinocentrism or Russocentrism that seeks to extend the countries' existing internal political order outward, and anti-hegemonism. Although Russian nationalism includes a strain of xenophobia that fueled demagoguery against China in the 1990s, Putin has sharply restricted that aspect of it and avoids direct references to China's rise. Sinocentrist ideology has similarly tended to fuel tensions with Russia—including by challenging Russian claims in Central Asia, which had previously been part of the Soviet Union. But China's current leaders have shown, in international meetings and forums, including the Shanghai Cooperation Organization, that they are prepared to show deference to Russian political and cultural influence.

Second, China and Russia are underscoring their historical differences with the West and emphasizing their Cold War–era divide with the United States. Officially sanctioned writing in both countries makes scant mention of the Cold War Sino-Soviet dispute. Although some Chinese historians had previously acknowledged that the Korean War began because of North Korean aggression in South Korea, the latest textbooks universally blame the United States for the war. Likewise, policymakers and analysts in both countries increasingly argue that the West never changed its imperialist Cold War mindset (as evidenced by its alleged support for so-called color revolutions in Ukraine and Hong Kong). This rhetoric implies that China and Russia are still obliged to resist its influence and help create a new international order.

Third, both countries have argued that the global financial crisis of 2008 demonstrates that the West's economic and political model is on the verge of failure and inferior to their own models. (The latter half of this argument has resonated more in China than in Russia.) Leaders in both Beijing and Moscow have refused to allow civil society to pose a threat to their rule, cracking down more ruthlessly in 2014 than at any time since the beginning of the 1990s.

Fourth, Putin and Xi have emphasized the importance of Chinese-Russian bilateral relations in the face of outside threats. This is a corollary of both governments' emphasis on the importance of communism, whether as the currently reigning ideology (in China) or as a positive historical legacy (in Russia). This has left both countries with few natural ideological allies other than each other—and there is little reason to believe this will change in the foreseeable future.

Fifth, Russia and China have made a successful effort to stay on the same side in international disputes. Rather than clash openly over regional issues, such as Vietnam's territorial and energy policies, China and Russia have discouraged public discussion of their differences, thus minimizing public pressure in each country to stand up to the other. At the same time, each country has trumpeted the threat of the United States and its allies in any dispute that bears on either country. This campaign has been so effective that it was sometimes difficult this year to distinguish between Russian and Chinese writing on the Ukraine crisis or the Hong Kong demonstrations.

Sixth, there are official campaigns under way in both countries to promote national identity. Putin and Xi have used all the resources at their disposal, involving both tight censorship and intense, top-down argumentation, to mobilize their respective countries behind a shrill political narrative that justifies domestic repression and foreign repression. These appeals have been effective because they draw on historic grievances and use familiar chauvinistic rhetoric. The result in both countries has been the most significant spike in nationalism since the height of the Cold War.

China's rhetoric in support of Putin's actions in Ukraine and Russia's rhetoric endorsing Xi's thinking about East Asia is not a coincidence. Rather, it is a feature of a new, post–Cold War geopolitical order. As long as the current political elites in China and Russia hold on to power, there is no reason to expect a major shift in either country's national identity or in the Sino-Russian relationship. Countries hoping to create a divide between the two—including Japan under Prime Minister Shinzo Abe—are bound to be disappointed. It is no accident, in other words, that the United States has failed to win China's support against Russian expansionism in Ukraine. Whether the issue is North Korea, Iran, or some other challenge to the West, one should be prepared for more Sino-Russian competition, not less.

A Meeting of the Minds

Did Japan and China Just Press Reset?

J. Berkshire Miller

NOVEMBER 10, 2014

After months of back-channel diplomacy, Japanese Prime Minister Shinzo Abe and Chinese leader Xi Jinping finally met this week on the sidelines of the Asia-Pacific Economic Cooperation (APEC) summit in Beijing. The Abe-Xi meeting is long overdue and represents the first time the leaders from the world's second and third biggest economies have talked since Abe took office in December 2012. Beijing had simply refused to meet with Tokyo at the summit level ever since the previous Japanese administration made the ill-fated decision to purchase three of the disputed Senkaku (Diaoyu) Islands in September 2012.

It isn't only the Senkaku (Diaoyu) Islands dispute that has troubled relations between Beijing and Tokyo. China accuses Abe and his cabinet of historical revisionism, for one. Beijing points to Abe's visit to the Yasukuni Shrine—a Shinto shrine dedicated to Japan's war dead from a wide range of conflicts, from the Satsuma Rebellion to World War II—last December, along with repeated visits by several of his cabinet ministers, as proof that the current government wants to reinterpret the traditional narrative of Japanese culpability during World War II. Abe, meanwhile, has called out China for stoking international and nationalist sentiment

J. BERKSHIRE MILLER is Chair of the Japan-Korea Working Group at the Pacific Forum of the Center for Strategic and International Studies and a Fellow on East Asia at the EastWest Institute.

against Japan through its education system and its desire to politicize its troubled history with Japan. Similarly, Abe has railed against Beijing's repeated intrusions in the territorial waters around the Senkaku (Diaoyu) Islands as an affront to international law and a rules-based system.

The Abe-Xi meeting is thus a major breakthrough, and it comes mostly thanks to significant diplomatic pressure from Japan to hold such a meeting. For months, the Abe administration had sent former high-level Japanese politicians to Beijing as envoys. For example, just two weeks before the Abe-Xi meeting, Japan's former Prime Minister Yasuo Fukuda met with Xi on the heels of the Boao Forum for Asia held in Beijing. Similarly, Tokyo's new governor, Yoichi Masuzoe, met with Xi this past April. Fukuda's and Masuzoe's meetings with Xi came amid a flurry of other ad hoc sit-downs between Japanese politicians and senior Chinese leadership over the past several months.

Abe's insistence on talking to Xi dates to when he first took office. He declared at the time that he thought high-level dialogue was the best way to improve troubled bilateral ties. Nevertheless, even though Abe wanted to repair relations with Beijing, he was also determined to take a hard-line approach on the islands dispute and not be seen as caving in to Chinese pressure. So Abe has always insisted that there be no preconditions to talks, for example, something that was unacceptable to Beijing, which did not want to award Abe with a high-level meeting without concessions on history and the territorial row.

Last week, senior officials from both sides finally managed to come together on an agreed joint statement that paved the way for a bilateral summit at APEC. The statement declares that the two sides would continue to build a "mutually beneficial relationship based on common strategic interests." To finally bring Beijing to the table, it seems that Abe had to make two nuanced offers. First, Abe has likely given back-channel—although not official—assurances that he will not visit the Yasukuni Shrine for the remainder of his tenure as prime minister. Indeed, according to multiple reports in Japan, Fukuda relayed this pledge to Beijing during his trips to meet with Chinese officials over the past few months. The joint statement vaguely hints at this point, noting that both sides "shared some recognition that, following the spirit of squarely facing history and advancing toward the future, they would overcome political difficulties that affect their bilateral relations." The wording lacked an official pledge on Yasukuni—which would have been politically impossible for Abe—but did acquiesce to Beijing's request that Japan acknowledge the historical issues before a meeting.

Second, and more controversial, Abe has agreed to recognize that there is some form of disagreement in the East China Sea with Beijing, while still affirming Japan's long-stated line that the Senkaku (Diaoyu) Islands are inherent parts of Japanese territory. Specifically, Tokyo and Beijing agreed "they had different views as to the emergence of tense situations in recent years in the waters of the East China Sea, including those around the Senkaku Islands, and shared the view that, through dialogue and consultation, they would prevent the deterioration of the situation, establish a crisis management mechanism and avert the rise of unforeseen circumstances." The statement on the islands spat is significant, and although it might appear that Japan succumbed to Chinese pressure to admit there is a dispute, a closer look at the statement reveals that the only acknowledgment is that the two sides disagree. Indeed, the fact that Japan avoided any mention of sovereignty in the statement should be seen as a diplomatic win for Tokyo.

Abe's acknowledgment of a disagreement in the East China Sea, regardless of the wording, is a significant step forward on what has become a very dangerous flash point for the countries. Indeed, tensions had been slowly building in the East China Sea since the arrest of a Chinese fishing captain following his trawler's ramming of Japanese coast guard vessels in 2010. The subsequent 2012 purchase of three islands by the government of former Japanese Prime Minister Yoshihiko Noda prompted more Chinese assertiveness in the maritime space surrounding the disputed isles. Aside from dispatching coast guard and white-hulled commercial vessels, Beijing upped the stakes in the airspace above the islands through its introduction of reconnaissance planes and its unilateral imposition of an Air Defense Identification Zone in the East China Sea last November. Since that time, there have been repeated and sustained intrusions by Chinese ships and aircraft in the area.

With little communication or political dialogue between the countries, both sides have been concerned that an accidental clash around the islands could snowball. For now, things are calmer. Over the past six months, as Japan has been pushing hard to restore diplomatic ties with China, the number of reported intrusions, as outlined by the Japanese coast guard, around the territorial sea of the Senkaku (Diaoyu) Islands has dropped dramatically. For example, there were 188 such incidents in 2013; so far this year, there have been merely 64. Similarly, despite a recent surge in the number of Chinese vessels entering the contiguous zone around the islands—water adjacent to the territorial seas—there has been a relative decline since the previous year. Curiously, Beijing also avoided sending any vessels at all to the contiguous zone during a two-week period last month.

Government officials on both sides also met in Qingdao this September to agree to resume a working-level dialogue on improving crisis management tools for the dispute. In addition, there was a call to create a hot line for improved communications between both capitals, an idea that the joint statement preceding the summit effectively green-lighted. The resumption of the High-Level Consultation on Maritime Affairs in Qingdao in September is also critical because it involves a wide range of government stakeholders on both sides, including representatives from respective navies, coast guards, and fishery agencies, in addition to diplomatic and defense officials.

There has been some less noticed movement on nonsecurity issues as well, such as the attempt to resuscitate the Trilateral Cooperation Secretariat, which works on regional issues with South Korea. In September, senior diplomats from all three sides met in

Seoul to push forward negotiations for a China-Japan-Korea trilateral free trade agreement. Through the Trilateral Cooperation Secretariat, China and Japan have also met several times over the past year to discuss key environmental issues, including climate change and combating urban air pollution. The trilateral option, despite adding the problematic Japan-Korea relationship into the mix, would provide a unique vehicle for building cooperation without the political sensitivities associated with bilateral meetings.

The Abe-Xi summit at APEC predictably lacked any pomp or formal deliverables. But the symbolic importance of the meeting should not be underestimated. Breaking the two-year gridlock effectively signals that both governments have granted high-level approval—especially necessary in Beijing's case—for continuing efforts at the bureaucratic level to slowly repair ties. Yet it would be premature to view the move as a signal of détente between Japan and China, whose relationship is still marred by competing nationalisms, differing strategic visions for the region, and mistrust. Indeed, rather than increasing the chance of a formal summit between Abe and Xi the near future, the APEC meeting might delay it, since China could believe that it has already conceded enough to Japan. In this scenario, too, the incremental repair of bilateral ties would be left to respective diplomats on each side until a major breakthrough, such as a more comprehensive agreed-upon joint statement on the East China Sea, can be found. The coming months will determine how much compromise both sides are willing to accept in order to maintain this little bit of momentum.

Sect Supreme

The End of Realist Politics in the Middle East

Bassel F. Salloukh   JULY 14, 2014

The stunning recent military successes by the Islamic State in Iraq and al-Sham (ISIS) have triggered a wave of gloomy prognoses about the demise of the Sykes-Picot regional order in the Levant and the withering away of the Iraqi and Syrian territorial states. However, the stakes are higher than the disintegration of what have always been permeable borders and the collapse of a long bygone Anglo-French agreement. Indeed, this year could mark the birth of a new regional order, one that dismisses the all-too-realist geopolitical contests of the past and clings, instead, to sectarianism.

The trend toward sectarianism in otherwise realist geopolitical contests commenced shortly after the 2003 U.S. invasion and occupation of Iraq and has culminated, for now, in ISIS' blitzkrieg throughout the country. In other words, ISIS' gains are consecrating rather than creating the politicization of narrow and exclusionary sectarian, ethnic, religious, and tribal identities, which appeared to have weakened during the Arab Spring. Now many countries in the Arab world are starting to look like Lebanon—once considered an Arab anomaly—in which historically-constructed sectarian identities have been institutionalized and hardened by a consociational power-sharing arrangement. Over time, sectarian identities

BASSEL F. SALLOUKH is Associate Dean of the School of Arts and Sciences and Associate Professor of Political Science at the Lebanese American University (LAU).

across the region may, like in Lebanon, come to seem continuous and permanent. And if Lebanon's cyclical patterns of political crises, internal wars, and external interventions are any guide, that future won't be a pleasant one.

To be sure, the growing sectarian regional order has deep roots, for which authoritarianism is partly to blame. Liberal oligarchies briefly ruled the region after the collapse of the Ottoman Empire and the First World War. But they were short-lived. Due to the stress of the 1948 loss of Palestine, external interventions, and internal praetorian pressures, those regimes gave way to authoritarian ones that prioritized a centralized unitary state. That model ultimately concentrated political and coercive power in the hands of a family, sect, tribe, class, region, or a combination thereof, thus alienating and excluding other groups. The homogenizing regimes systematically discriminated against, among others, the Assyrians, Kurds, Shia, and Turkmen in Iraq; the southerners in Sudan and Yemen; the Berber communities in Algeria; the Kurds and rural Sunnis in Syria; the eastern Barqa province and the Amazigh, Tabu, and Tuareg minorities in Libya; the Bedoon (stateless) in Kuwait; the Shia in Bahrain and Saudi Arabia; the Copts in Egypt; and the Palestinians in Jordan.

Hindsight is always 20/20, but imagine that post-independence Arab states had been built on the idea of inclusive civic citizenship. Perhaps then they would not have faced such frequent and violent demands for secession, decentralization, federalism, and confederalism. Sudan's rupture into two states was an extreme case, and probably not the best regional precedent because it encouraged other groups to follow a similar path, as with the Kurds in Iraq who now deny the existence of an Iraqi identity and boldly insist on independence. Far better examples are Yemen's new federal institutional structure, which, despite some internal contradictions, at least avoids perpetual war along tribal, sectarian, and regional lines. Even in tiny Lebanon, most Maronites, who at first wanted their own country and whose Church and political elites later lobbied the authorities of the French mandate to create a Greater Lebanon, now prefer autonomous self-governing districts and broad administrative and political decentralization.

But the growing regional order isn't all based on history. More recent geopolitical battles have also played a role. In the early days after Tunisia and Egypt's authoritarian regimes broke down, a new kind of politics seemed to be emerging. Protestors opted for non-violence, reimagining their public duties as citizens in the pursuit of a new political community built on democracy, social justice, and economic opportunity. Smooth democratic transitions proved elusive, however, not because of a presumed Arab cultural aversion to democracy, but rather because of oil, geopolitics, and the lingering effects of the Arab–Israeli conflict.

Tunisia is the exception that proves the rule. Its political parties heroically put the country's democratic transition back on track after domestic Islamist and transnational Salafi-Jihadist alike derailed it by, respectively, replicating the authoritarian regime's exclusionary practices, and using violence to terrorize their secular political opponents. Yet, Tunisia's democratic transition is also the product of some unique structural features. Tunisia has no hydrocarbon reserves and no borders with Israel, and it happens to be outside the arena where post-2003 geopolitical battles have been fought. These overlapping factors have made it possible for Tunisian political actors to renegotiate the terms of their democratic transition free from the exigencies of international strategic calculations and regional geopolitical battles.

By contrast, geopolitics transformed what commenced as a genuine nonviolent reform movement in Syria into a domestic, regional, and international struggle for Syria. For years, the grand Saudi-Iranian competition for regional dominance has played out in Iraq, Lebanon, the West Bank and Gaza Strip, and, to a lesser extent, in Yemen and Bahrain. In Syria, it found a new site, one that would prove to be a game-changer. Riyadh sought to oust the Bashar al-Assad regime in Syria to contain Iran's regional influence. Not to be outmaneuvered, Tehran sent in its most trusted Iraqi and Lebanese proxies under the supervision of Revolutionary

Guard commanders. Hezbollah's subsequent involvement in Syria may have obviated regime collapse, protected the party's operational and logistic routes to Iran, and saved it from being encircled by Israel and becoming beholden to Saudi Arabia. In doing so, it has also galvanized sectarian sentiments across the region, and exposed the party's own constituency to waves of suicide attacks by Salafi-Jihadi groups. The war for Syria simply magnified the use of sectarianism in the region's realist geopolitical battles, but with destructive and long-term reverberations.

The battle between Riyadh and Tehran all but destroyed Syria's state institutions and much of its intricate social fabric. It exposed societal divisions that had been camouflaged by decades of populism. After all, weak states give rise to strong factions, and sectarian and other communal identities thrive as the state crumbles. Local and transnational militant groups, including ISIS, mushroomed and filled the consequent institutional and ideological void created by the collapse of state institutions. Once those groups were formed, it was only a matter of time before they crossed the border. Iraqi Prime Minister Nouri al-Maliki's stubbornly sectarian administration alienated Iraq's Sunni population and unified otherwise strange bedfellows—namely ISIS and the remnants of Saddam's Baathist military and coercive intelligence apparatus—in the battle against a presumed common Shia enemy.

In other words, those who now claim that U.S. President Barack Obama "lost Iraq" by ignoring Maliki's creeping sectarianism miss the larger and more complete picture: Ever since the 2003 U.S. invasion, the geopolitical battles between Riyadh and Tehran have been waged with the help of the stealth weapon of sectarian agitation. Well before Obama's tenure, but also during his presidency, Washington even condoned the politicization of sectarianism when it served its own regional interests—as in the post-2005 attempt to drown Hezbollah in a Lebanese sectarian quagmire. Other times, it opted to sit idle as its regional enemies were locked in a mutually destructive battle in Syria. As the German philosopher Arthur Schopenhauer might quip, sectarianism is not a policy that one can condone or condemn at will. Moreover, the United States' regional allies played an instrumental role in flooding Syria with Salafi-Jihadi fighters from all over the world. The sectarianism unleashed in the region by these fighters is as unprecedented as it is destructive. Instead of forcing its allies to close the pipelines, Washington was busy creating typologies of the different groups fighting in Syria. These typologies have now proved useless; neither the United States nor any other European state will be immune from the blowback effects of the bizarre strategy of regime change in Syria.

In the growing new regional order, it is not so much the territorial borders of the Arab states that the rest of the world should worry about. Rather, it is their unstable internal political configurations. Unfortunately, the popular uprisings of the Arab Spring may prove to be a brief hiatus between two equally undesirable regional orders: the era of the homogenizing unitary authoritarian Arab state and that of sectarian identity, presumably primordial but actually historically-constructed and modern, in the context of fractured statelets or regions assembled into weak states. Only the negotiation of new socioeconomic and political power-sharing pacts based on the principles of fairness and mutual recognition can help forestall this grim scenario. However, it is not too late for Washington to lead a region-wide grand bargain that could find a balance between the geopolitical interests of the regional powers and the aspirations of the region's peoples. This entails consistent and proactive U.S. efforts to stabilize Arab states and end sectarian geopolitical battles by helping local actors renegotiate the emerging regional order's new spheres of interest. Geopolitical battles are nothing new to the Middle East's regional order; their sectarianization is, however, and it has proven destructive for the states and societies of the region. Washington cannot base its policies on the selective binaries and contradictions that have defined and marred its approach for the last few years. The mayhem that awaits the region without new power-sharing pacts and a robust regional bargain will make any talk of the Sykes-Picot agreement and the political order it once gave birth to seem quaint.

The Middle East's Durable Map

Rumors of Sykes-Picot's Death are Greatly Exaggerated

Steven Simon   AUGUST 26, 2014

J ust as hysteria about the demise of Sykes-Picot was starting to
die down, the Islamic State of Iraq and al-Sham (ISIS) has revived it by declaring its intention to revive the caliphate at
least over what is now Iraqi and Syrian territory. The news arrived
in two separate ISIS videos, one featuring a Chechen militant pre-
siding over the dismantling of an outpost on the Syrian-Iraqi border and the other showcasing an English-speaking Chilean jihadist.

Amid the post–Arab Spring everything-has-changed anxiety,
fears that Syria's dismemberment would lead to the unraveling of
all the hard work that Sir Mark Sykes and François Georges-
Picot did back in 1916–17 have loomed large. The civil war in
Syria seemed to presage the breakup of the state and the rejigger-
ing of its borders to serve Iraqi Sunni, Israeli, Lebanese, Kurdish,
and Turkish purposes. Ankara, for example, had threatened to
seize the Syrian city of Idlib if refugee flows out of the country
exceeded a very low threshold, which has long since been crossed.
Syria's Kurds, meanwhile, were expected to cordon off their part
of Syria from the rest of the country and then join Iraqi Kurdistan in declaring independence. Along the Lebanese-Syrian border, Hezbollah was expected to expand its territory at Syria's

STEVEN SIMON is Senior Fellow at the Middle East Institute in Washington, D.C.

expense to preserve lines of communication to a coastal Alawite enclave if Assad lost control of the rest of the country. And, if Israel felt threatened by radical Sunnis in Syria, the thinking went, it might want to push its existing boundaries in the Golan Heights eastward to establish a kind of buffer zone between the interior and Israeli towns on the escarpment. Above all, there was a fear that the Iraqi-Syrian border would crumble, as it eventually did. Indeed, anxiety about Sykes-Picot seemed to raise the stakes of the civil war in Syria, intensifying dread about a broader Middle East meltdown.

Thus far, however, the parade of horrors emanating from Syria has not included the demise of Sykes-Picot borders. The Turks have not taken a bite out of Syria, although they have helped undermine its eventual reconstitution by incubating ISIS. Syrian Kurds have not proposed—or implemented—new borders, and their Iraqi counterparts have refrained from secession or the formalization of their de facto autonomy. Hezbollah has not picked up any new territory, even as the Syrian regime's disintegration has threatened Hezbollah's lifeline to Iran. Israel has certainly taken advantage of anarchic conditions in Syria to strike targets of opportunity, but it hasn't made any decisive attempt to carve out a *cordon sanitaire*. And, before it was breached by ISIS, the Iraqi-Syrian border had been permeable for generations, owing to the nature of the terrain and the large tribal confederations on either side whose economic interests require that the border not impede their movements.

In short, despite the regional pandemonium, Sykes-Picot seems to be alive and well.

Although the border between Iraq and Syria might be near the vanishing point, there are boundaries that still mean something.

That shouldn't be surprising. Land borders settled via negotiation, especially when sealed by treaty, tend to be stable, even where relations between the neighboring states remain volatile or even hostile. The reason? Questioning settled boundaries inevitably invites nettlesome counterclaims, especially in regions where ethnic or tribal groups straddle borders and minority populations have ended up behind the lines when the maps were finalized.

Fortunately for the Middle East, most of its borders were settled by treaty. Admittedly, there are a couple of major exceptions. Israel's borders remain in flux. There isn't a Palestinian state or a final status accord, so a border between Israel and the West Bank isn't possible to determine, even if many observers are fairly sure of what shape that border will eventually take. On the Lebanese side, Israel had been content to occupy a swath of southern Lebanon for long periods without ever proposing border alterations, even when Israeli Prime Minister David Ben-Gurion had contemplated them in the 1950, according to his foreign minister Moshe Sharett. (Syria likewise occupied large parts of Lebanon until April 2005 without tampering with the de facto border set by the French mandate in 1920.) Israel's formal annexation of the Golan Heights in December 1981 did not result in the establishment of a new international border, nor did it foreclose future Israeli attempts to negotiate Golan's return to Syria in exchange for a variety of concessions, apparently including, most recently, an end to Syria's strategic relationship with Iran. By contrast, Israel's borders with both Egypt and Jordan were settled by treaty and there is nothing to suggest that the parties regard them as anything but inviolable.

There are, of course, other major exceptions that prove the general rule of border stability. The border between the Yemen Arab Republic and the People's Democratic Republic of Yemen was erased upon the unification of the country in 1990. But this merely corrected a historical anomaly in which one part of the country was granted independence after World War I while the other remained a British colony until 1967. A more dramatic exception was Iraq's 1980 invasion of Iran, which aimed to seize Iranian territory. But even that was the culmination of a series of border disputes and, therefore, less than surprising. Likewise, Saddam Hussein's conquest of Kuwait in 1990 was premised in part on the allegedly inimical role Great Britain had played in setting the boundary between Kuwait and Iraq in the 1920s. Until the British arrived on the scene, the line had been ill-defined because the Ottoman government was not overly concerned with where Basra ended and Kuwait began.

Evidently, it takes more than a devastating civil war in Syria—or, even before that, the liberation of the Kurds as a result of the U.S. invasion of Iraq—to chip away at the granite base of the Sykes-Picot monument. Pessimists, however, have now identified a new threat to the old map: jihadism, as embodied by ISIS.

It is undeniable that transnational jihadism is the most dynamic political movement in the Middle East and North Africa, and it is the one form of durable political self-expression that can be said to have emerged from the Arab uprisings of 2010–11. It is not a monolithic force, of course, but ISIS' terrifying return to Iraq from the battlefields of Syria does recall the newly Islamicized Arab tribes from the Arabian desert that flowed into the Levant in the mid-seventh century and scattered the Byzantine armies before them as they redrew the regional map. But the notion that even ISIS could erase all regional borders is just not very plausible, in part because the group is confined to the box built by Sykes-Picot.

Although the border between Iraq and Syria might be near the vanishing point, there are boundaries that still mean something. After all, where is ISIS supposed to go next? Ankara, by whose kindness ISIS has thus far thrived, is perfectly capable of keeping the group out of Anatolia. In fact, it seems to have already begun closing those border gates. Kurdistan, too, is out of bounds thanks to the help that the United States, France, and possibly others have provided Kurdish forces. The Saudis, with U.S. help, can certainly keep ISIS out of the Kingdom. Kuwait, which remains a staging base for the U.S. military, is likewise a hard target. To even get to either destination, ISIS would have to fight through Baghdad and the Shia heartland. That, too, seems implausible. ISIS could try to invade Jordan, but the Jordanian army is more capable than most in the Middle East and can depend on both U.S. support (in December, the United States deployed 6,000 troops to the country for a major combined exercise with Jordanian forces) and, in a pinch,

Israeli military help to counter an ISIS Barbarossa. Lebanon, given its perpetually volatile politics, is vulnerable to ISIS-inspired subversion and attack. But it is a small place and its internal security service is pervasive—two conditions that constrain potential attackers. Looking eastward, the notion that Iran, which took hundreds of thousands of casualties in repelling an Iraqi juggernaut in the 1980s, is going to melt in terror in the face of several thousand ISIS brigands is absurd. As a geopolitical reality, it is hard to imagine ISIS flooding across the region the way Nazi armies did across Europe during the opening credits of *Casablanca*.

There is also the matter of capabilities. Granted, ISIS has accumulated battlefield experience, which shows in its operations. After a fashion, it can manage to operate and maintain the heavy weapons it captured from Syrian stocks. But the group probably won't be able to do the same for the more complicated U.S. gear captured from Iraqi forces. Its barbarism has been effective at terrorizing civilians and shattering the morale of poorly led, inexperienced, and exhausted Iraq troops. But they cannot mass without exposing themselves to air attack, and ISIS air defenses are minimal. As the rapid retreat of ISIS from the Mosul Dam indicated, U.S. aircraft can lacerate ISIS when its fighters come out in numbers on the offensive, or stop to set up mortar or artillery positions.

From the perspective of ISIS' adversaries, air power isn't a perfect military solution, since it delivers outright victory only when combined with ground operations that the United States has ruled out and at this stage, Iraqi forces aren't ready to carry out. In military terms, then, ISIS still has some maneuvering room within the larger geopolitical limits that confine it. The group's advances in Raqqa, Syria demonstrate this all too clearly. Nevertheless, capabilities are also a question of numbers. In Syria, ISIS has an advantage because of the preponderance of Sunnis in the overall population, but the regime has proven itself capable in counterinsurgency. In Iraq, ISIS is at an ethnic disadvantage, which over the long haul will offset the Iraqi military's current inadequacies.

Furthermore, ISIS' tactical skill exceeds its strategic savvy. The militants' battlefield gains notwithstanding, their self-confidence, sense of mission, and jihadist ardor have led them to overreach. ISIS has heightened anxieties in Ankara, Baghdad, Erbil, Riyadh, and Tehran, which have forged a tacit anti-ISIS alliance. Saudi and Iranian concurrence to select a replacement for Iraqi Prime Minister Nouri al-Maliki is one example. A recent Iranian overture to Kurdistan is another. None of this is meant to suggest that ISIS' days are numbered—only that its prospects are limited.

ISIS does have a potent cross-border ideological appeal. It is, after all, fighting the Assad regime in Syria and has chalked up some striking victories against Iraqi Shia. The swift viral spread of the video of James Foley's beheading will no doubt burnish this reputation. A successful, popular Arab army, especially one seen to be humiliating the United States, must be a galvanizing sight for a young population with meager resources and a bleak future. Unrest precipitated in regional cities by ISIS exploits can really only be dealt with by good governance that generates jobs and improves living conditions in teeming, filthy cities undergirded by over-whelmed and deteriorating infrastructures. State capacity to do this is obviously limited, but regional governments, having faced al Qaeda's challenge for years, are aware of the political dynamics and the need to respond as effectively as possible. In vulnerable countries, particularly in Jordan, religious parties—including Salafists and Muslim Brothers—are trying to counter the appeal of ISIS-style activism by disparaging the group as heretical, invoking patriotism, portraying ISIS as anti-Islamic, and casting it as an existential threat.

The rise of ISIS is also clearly exciting for the thousands of European, American, and other foreign fighters that have flocked to its banner. Upon their return to their countries of origin, some may mount terrorist operations in ISIS' name. But in this vein ISIS constitutes a counterterrorism and homeland security problem, and not even as formidable a threat as al Qaeda vintage 9/11, which unlike ISIS had trained and prepared for covert operations. In any case, ISIS' out-of-area threat is no more likely to affect borders within the region than al Qaeda's has done for the past twenty years.

The advent of ISIS as a force to be reckoned with in the Middle East is immensely regrettable, and there is relatively little the United States alone can do about it. Even so, the group is unlikely to determine the legacy of Sykes and Picot, much less the longer term future of the Middle East.

Staying Out of Syria

Why the United States Shouldn't Enter the Civil War—But Why It Might Anyway

Steven Simon OCTOBER 26, 2014

U.S. President Barack Obama has taken pains to avoid being drawn into Syria's civil war. He does not appear convinced that the United States has sufficient strategic interests in Syria to warrant—let alone sustain—another long-term commitment of military force to shape the outcome of what is a complicated and many-sided struggle. Even as Obama has expanded the U.S. war against the Islamic State of Iraq and al-Sham (ISIS) to include targets in Syria, then, he has tried to circumscribe the mission. The aim is to battle ISIS without either aiding or fighting the regime of Syrian President Bashar al-Assad. But the balancing act is proving difficult. The United States could soon face a choice between appearing to provide tacit support to Syrian government forces and joining the fight against them.

The United States has long faced pressure to intervene in Syria's civil war; it dates back to 2011, even before early skirmishes turned into high-intensity combat. Then as now, the administration's stance was cautious. At that stage, it looked as though Assad might go the way of Tunisia's Zine el-Abidine Ben Ali or Egypt's Hosni Mubarak. Given the brittleness of the Assad regime, the use of force seemed unnecessary. And in any case, there was no appetite for a bidding war with Iran for Syria.

STEVEN SIMON is Senior Fellow at the Middle East Institute in Washington, D.C.

Yet the Assad regime proved more resilient than many expected. Interest in arming and training the Syrian rebels only grew, despite Washington's evident inability to wield influence over the hundreds of partially radicalized armed groups already proliferating in Syria, let alone mold them into a unified opposition army. As we now know from multiple memoirs, Obama overruled his secretaries of defense and state, who urged him to do more to arm those rebels in late 2012.

Calls to help overthrow Assad grew louder after his regime used chemical weapons against civilian populations in August 2013. Again, Obama declined to strike once the United Kingdom opted out of military involvement and Russia proffered a diplomatic alternative that eventually stripped the regime of its chemical weapons. The resulting mix of disappointment and anger at home over a forgone opportunity to strike Assad's forces was bound to make it harder for Obama to say no the next time a challenge arose.

The key question is: What happens if one of the non-jihadist opposition groups that the United States is aiding in the fight against ISIS requests urgent assistance against the Assad regime?

And it did. Following reports that ISIS, which had just overrun the western provinces of Iraq and entered Mosul, was intent on the genocide of a religious minority in Iraq, the United States immediately launched air strikes to protect the vulnerable and safeguard American officials in Erbil. The use of force never comes without unintended consequences, and in this case, the attacks precipitated the murder of two Americans, which in turn amplified calls for military escalation.

Even so, in that early phase of U.S. military operations, the air campaign was in the service of a clear, if limited, interest in protecting the American strategic investment in Iraq by relieving jihadist pressure on Baghdad and pushing the divisive prime minister, Nouri al-Maliki, out of office. To the extent that prospective strikes in Syria were discussed, their narrow aim was to deprive what was seen as an Iraqi insurgency of its sanctuary across the border. As the objective expanded to include the destruction of

ISIS, though, U.S. strikes have extended as far west as the out-skirts of Syria's former cultural and economic capital of Aleppo, now a vast rubble field contested by the regime and a congeries of rebel militias, and as far north as the Turkish border.

These attacks, with their implied promise of close air support for non-jihadist fighters assailed by ISIS, have brought the United States perilously close to entry into the Syrian civil war. Turkish Prime Minister Ahmet Davutoglu's recent offer to send Turkish troops into Syria if the United States would, in return, directly at-tack the Assad regime—and Ankara's wrangling with the United States over access to Turkish air bases—has only added to sustained pressure coming from the Gulf allies.

The key question is: What happens if one of the non-jihadist opposition groups that the United States is aiding in the fight against ISIS requests urgent assistance against the Assad regime? If the United States fails to come to the group's aid, the support the United States enjoys among these groups by virtue of its airpower and train-and-equip efforts would swiftly fade. But if the United States accedes to the request, then it unequivocally becomes a com-batant in the civil war. And if the United States consents to Tur-key's proposal for a safe haven within Syria for refugees and possibly as a base for an opposition army—essentially a tethered goat stratagem designed to trigger regime attacks that American planes would then have to repel—Washington would become even more deeply engaged in the conflict.

The civil war in Syria does, of course, endanger some U.S. stra-tegic interests. Iraq, for example, is one, and the United States has acted decisively to protect it. Jordan is another, given the Hashem-ite Kingdom's historically close relationship with the United States (it is a Major non-NATO Ally) and its close security links to Israel. The influx of Syrian refugees into that country is a threat to its stability, as is the receptive audience ISIS has found among the unemployed youth in its impoverished desert cities. In response, the United States ramped up its already considerable economic and military aid to Jordan and, last December, deployed 6,000 soldiers to Jordan for a large-scale exercise. Likewise, Lebanon has received billions in military aid from Riyadh, while Hezbollah fields a force that has faced the Israeli army on the battlefield and is ideologically primed to contest ISIS attempts to establish a beachhead in Lebanon. And between 2012 and now, the United States has provided nearly $3 billion in humanitarian aid for displaced Syrians.

But there is no equivalent U.S. interest in Syria per se. For 40 years, it was a strategic ally of the Soviets; it then switched its allegiance to another strategic adversary, Iran. Most Syrians are skeptical of U.S. intentions, owing to decades of support for Israel as well as the United States' hands-off approach to the civil war. Assad's outreach to Washington, which came only a short time before rebellion broke out, was too little, too late. There is no history of cooperation, shared causes, or solemn commitments. Syria is of no military value to the United States, which has ample basing and access options throughout the Mediterranean rim, and of negligible economic value.

It would be strategically useful to completely deny Syrian territory to Iran, but the attempt to do so would likely increase Iran's military involvement and heighten sectarian tensions, while complicating efforts to reach a deal on Iran's nuclear program. Although some terrorist attacks in the West, such as the one just carried out in Canada, will certainly arise from a jihadized Syria, the long-term investment the United States has made in homeland security and intelligence programs, combined with air strikes that keep ISIS conspirators in Syria and Iraq off balance, should contain the problem without the burden of a new expeditionary commitment.

Hence the administration's dilemma. On the one hand, military intervention in the civil war would commit the United States to an expensive and ongoing enterprise unrelated to a strategic interest in Syria itself. On the other, it might prove necessary in order to bring other countries' firepower to bear against ISIS. While Washington debates the question, however, its air operations deep in Syrian territory could propel the United States into the civil war without a considered or explicit decision.

A tragic choice is emerging between restraint against ISIS to avoid entanglement in Syria's civil war or full engagement against ISIS with an eye to regime change and the reconstruction and stabilization of a devastated country. After Afghanistan, Iraq, and Libya, we have a rough idea of what such an effort would entail and of the elusiveness of lasting gains. A decision to go all the way is one that should be taken only with the greatest of caution and a careful assessment of the gap between our resources and our maximalist goals and the gap between these goals and our strategic interests. At this stage, all these considerations remain badly out of sync and quite possibly irreconcilable.

The Hollow Coalition

Washington's Timid European Allies

Raphael Cohen and
Gabriel Scheinmann   NOVEMBER 5, 2014

T hree months since U.S. bombs first struck Islamic State of Iraq and al-Sham (ISIS) targets in Iraq, the Obama administration has touted its 62-country coalition as a crowning achievement. Although this number might seem impressive, however, it is misleading. Of the 62 nominal allies for Operation Inherent Resolve (as the campaign is now called), only 16 have actually committed military forces, and only 11 have conducted offensive operations to date. Many appear willing to pay lip service to U.S. President Barack Obama's condemnation of ISIS, only to ignore his subsequent call to arms.

Most disconcerting is the meekness of Washington's supposedly stalwart European allies. The European countries that have deployed forces to fight ISIS are contributing less today than they did three years ago in Operation Unified Protector in Libya—and even in that conflict, the United States was indispensable to the mission. France is a case in point. It fired the opening shot in the Libyan campaign and sent to the front 29 planes and six warships, including an aircraft carrier. Today, however, it has devoted only 11 planes and one warship to fighting ISIS. Similarly, the United Kingdom sent 28 planes to Libya in 2011 but only eight to Iraq this year. And whereas a total of 13 European countries had

RAPHAEL COHEN and GABRIEL SCHEINMANN are defense analysts in Washington, D.C.

contributed either ships or planes to the struggle against the Muammar al-Qaddafi regime, only five have done the same in the war on ISIS.

Nowhere is European reticence more apparent than in the share of airstrikes. In Libya, 90 percent of the air raids were carried out by Washington's coalition partners, destroying more than 6,000 targets. This percentage puts the U.S. allies' current share—approximately 10 percent of over 800 strikes conducted so far in Iraq and Syria—to shame. The share of the EU is even smaller, since some strikes were conducted by other coalition partners: Australia, Canada, and five Arab states. And this time around, the European countries are openly admitting that their contribution would be mere window-dressing. As British Foreign Secretary Philip Hammond acknowledged in a particularly candid testimony in early September, the British contribution aimed primarily at bolstering "a political coalition of nations" rather than changing the military tide. Seventy years after British and American soldiers landed in nearly equal numbers on the beaches of Normandy, even the United Kingdom, which has Europe's most powerful military, recognizes that it can no longer be decisive on the battlefield.

SLIMMING THE RANKS

Such an underwhelming European response is puzzling. After all, European security interests should dictate an even more robust effort against ISIS than against the Qaddafi regime. For one, ISIS represents a much more immediate security threat. An estimated 3,000 European jihadists have joined ISIS' ranks, and many of them have returned home bent on further violence, including one that killed four people in an attack on the Jewish Museum of Belgium in Brussels this past May. Second, ISIS militants, unlike Qaddafi, have explicitly threatened to attack European countries and have killed European citizens. The Qaddafi regime, on the other hand, had signed a number of lucrative oil deals with European companies before it fell; it also largely abandoned its unconventional weapons program and ended its sponsorship of terrorism in Europe. And third, unlike the United States, Europe was mostly spared the Iraq war's direct toll (accounting for just 282 of the 4,804 coalition casualties, most borne by the United Kingdom) and therefore does not suffer from battle fatigue.

The reason for the European countries' lackluster effort lies not in their war weariness or a miscalculation of their interests but in their vastly diminished military capacity—the result of deep cuts to their defense budgets. Put simply, Washington's European allies no longer have the strength to conduct and sustain even medium-sized military operations.

Europe's military spending plummeted after the Cold War, and the recent recession has prompted five consecutive years of further cuts in absolute terms. The defense budgets of most NATO nations now stand at their lowest point since 2001, according to the Stockholm International Peace Research Institute. Currently, only Estonia, Greece, and the United Kingdom meet NATO's mutually agreed-upon target for defense spending—defined as two percent of GDP—even though member states reaffirmed their commitment to that target at a NATO summit in September. In 2013, European NATO members (a group that includes Turkey) spent a combined $270 billion on defense, which is less than half of the annual U.S. defense budget. As a result, the United States will likely dedicate more money to Operation Inherent Resolve than the majority of European NATO states will allocate to security and defense in the whole year.

NOT ON TARGET

The Libyan campaign, which some observers have praised as an example of European military effectiveness and used to urge more European involvement in Syria, represents just the opposite. In fact, it underscores Europe's declining military clout by demonstrating that EU countries can mount a successful military operation only under a best-case scenario. Cases that, like Iraq and Syria today, present greater strategic and logistic challenges quickly bring Europe's vulnerabilities to the fore.

Several factors combined to make Libya the perfect staging ground for a European military intervention. First, the operation took place just off the European coast, well within the range of European air bases. By contrast, to strike ISIS targets, European planes must fly out of Cyprus, Jordan, and the Persian Gulf countries—a far more difficult task from the logistical and diplomatic standpoints. Second, Libya's vast stretches of open desert between population centers made for an easier operating environment. Although western Iraq is likewise sparsely populated, ISIS strongholds such as the cities of Mosul (in northern Iraq) and Raqqa (in Syria) are not. Finally, unlike Qaddafi's army, which had lost its edge long before the West intervened, ISIS fighters are well funded, well armed, and able to score impressive victories.

Yet even in that favorable situation, European countries found their logistic and intelligence capabilities stretched to the limit, forcing them to rely on U.S. forces. Noting these shortfalls, the 2013 edition of *The Military Balance,* an annual assessment of global defense capabilities published by the International Institute for Strategic Studies, concluded that the Libyan operation highlighted Europe's military decline rather than heralding Europe's emergence as a capable security actor.

Furthermore, after the initial victory in Libya, it quickly became clear that the Western operation there was not a success. Libya is in a state of anarchy. Its capital has fallen to Islamist militant factions, its parliament has fled, and its oil production hovers far below prewar levels. Meanwhile, nearby European countries are struggling to stem the tide of refugees streaming across Libyan borders. As just one example, Italy plans to discontinue its yearlong search-and-rescue operation in the central Mediterranean, which has saved the lives of more than 150,000 migrants. Its place will be taken by the new Operation Triton, funded by eight member states and intended to "ensure effective border control." In other words, only three years after they intervened to save Libyans from oppression, the European nations find themselves focused on keeping those same individuals out.

A whole array of other factors strengthens Europe's reluctance to enter such conflicts in the future. The EU is saddled by debt (with an average debt-to-GDP ratio of 88 percent) and faces declining birth rates and graying populations, forcing governments to devote funds to caring for their retirees rather than modernizing armies. Further, growing political discord at home—including a rise of far-right eurosceptic political parties—makes European leaders even more reluctant to join costly international military endeavors. Even new threats, such as ISIS or an armed separatist rebellion in eastern Ukraine, are likely to pale in comparison with Europe's other problems.

A SPENT FORCE

The disappointing European contribution to Operation Inherent Resolve offers several lessons. The tepid response highlights just how far European military capabilities have deteriorated. Even though some states have made modest increases to their defense budgets in response to Russia's actions in Ukraine, these changes fall far short of reversing Europe's military decline. The continued stagnation of European economies, dismal demographic trends, and lack of political will make the resurrection of Europe as a military power nearly impossible for the foreseeable future.

For that reason, the United States ought to reevaluate its future expectations of European military contributions, especially to out-of-area missions, and begin planning accordingly. With time, European states will become even less forthcoming with their military support. Washington's European allies simply lack the capability to contribute in a meaningful way, even in response to worthy military missions or security challenges on their doorstep. Washington should thus focus on enlisting allies that are not only willing to join a coalition but capable of contributing resources and personnel to it.

Finally, the war on ISIS underscores Washington's unique global position of leadership when it comes to defending the West. Its allies count on it to project power globally and even to come to their aid when they cannot defend themselves. For all its budget woes, political gridlock, and desire to pivot away from the world's problems, the United States will continue to find itself doing the heavy lifting—whether combating ISIS or deterring a recidivist Russia—for the foreseeable future. Simply put, there is no one else.

This is What Détente Looks Like

The United States and Iran Join Forces Against ISIS

Mohsen Milani   AUGUST 27, 2014

I t is no particular surprise that U.S. President Barack Obama is on the verge of turning over a new leaf with Iran. After all, over the course of his presidency, Obama has repeatedly emphasized that he would like the United States and Iran to overcome their 35 years of estrangement. What is surprising, however, is how rapprochement has come about—not through negotiations over the fate of Tehran's nuclear program, but as a result of the battle against ISIS.

Tehran and Washington find themselves on the same side in the fight against the Islamic State of Iraq and al-Sham (ISIS), also called the Islamic State (IS), and there are already signs that they have been cooperating against the extremist group's advance through Iraq. Although there is no guarantee that this will last for the duration of the war, such cooperation is clearly a positive step.

The United States and Iran both view ISIS as a significant threat to their own interests. An ISIS stronghold near the Iranian border would be a profound and immediate security threat to Tehran. For one, the Sunni jihadists of ISIS are openly disdainful of the Shia faith, the sect of Islam that the overwhelming majority of

MOHSEN MILANI is Professor of Politics and the Executive Director of the Center for Strategic and Diplomatic Studies at the University of South Florida. Follow him on Twitter @mohsenmilani.

Iranians and the majority of Iraqis adhere to. The group is already in a sectarian war in Syria and Iraq, and Tehran must assume that it eventually plans on turning its attention to Iran.

Washington, for its part, has also concluded that ISIS poses a significant threat. If ISIS manages to create a safe haven in Iraq, it could use the territory to plan operations against the West, undermine Western allies in the region, and endanger oil shipments in the Persian Gulf. In the meantime, the group's war against the Iraqi state also poses a danger to U.S. interests. Over the past decade, Washington has paid a high price in blood and treasure to create a stable and relatively friendly Iraq. The collapse of that state would be a humiliating defeat.

Although the United States and Iran have different visions for the future of Iraq, they share three major strategic goals there: protecting Iraq's territorial integrity; preventing a sectarian civil war that could easily metastasize into the entire region; and defeating ISIS. There is also a precedent of tactical cooperation in Iraq between Tehran and Washington: In 2001, the two cooperated to dislodge the Taliban from Afghanistan.

Obama has pledged not to tolerate the establishment of a terrorist state in Iraq and has already ordered limited air strikes against ISIS to protect U.S. personnel and facilities in Iraq and provide humanitarian relief to that country's desperate Yezidi minority. Tehran has given unambiguous signals that it approves of Obama's limited military mission. Iranian President Hassan Rouhani and a host of other officials have publicly expressed willingness to collaborate with the United States to defeat ISIS. It is unlikely that Tehran will offer tactical assistance to the United States on the battlefield, of course, but it is likely to welcome continued U.S. air strikes and might even quietly applaud the reintroduction of U.S. ground troops to Iraq.

But Obama has also declared, correctly, that there can't be a U.S. military solution for Iraq's problems until its political problems—above all, its central government's tendency toward exclusivism—have been addressed. This is where Iran, which has maintained very close ties with the Shia parties that are dominant in Baghdad, has taken the lead. Washington has greeted the arrival of Iraq's new prime minister, Haider al-Abadi. Abadi's predecessor, Nouri al-Maliki, only stepped down after Iran (and Ayatollah Ali Sistani, Iraq's leading Shia cleric) firmly pushed him to go. Tehran initially expressed its desire for Maliki to leave office in private. But when he still showed no signs of exiting, Ali Shamkhani, Secretary of Iran's Supreme National Security Council, issued a public declaration congratulating Abadi for being named to form a new government. Tehran also mobilized Iraqi Shia groups as well as Shia militias to support Abadi. Washington was reduced to being an observer in much of this process, but it welcomed the outcome.

The cooperation between Tehran and Washington in Iraq has been productive so far, but it is also fragile. There are three factors that could easily derail it. The first is a dispute over the composition of the new Iraqi government. Iran recognized that Maliki had become too polarizing and authoritarian a figure, but that does not mean that it has otherwise revised its strategy that Iraq's Shia community should dominate Iraqi politics, or changed its view that Sunni groups need to learn to accept Shia rule. As I wrote in an earlier article for *Foreign Affairs*, this is both a matter of principle (Shias comprise a comfortable majority of the Iraqi population) and pragmatism (Tehran believes that the Sunnis are less likely than the Shias and Kurds to be interested in building close ties with Iran).

Washington, by contrast, believes that Iraq's Shia community should wield less power than it naturally would under strict proportionality according to population. In part, this may be because of pressure from Sunni governments in the region, including Saudi Arabia. But the United States also believes that some of Iraq's Shia groups are more interested in acquiring a monopoly over national power than wielding power in a responsible fashion.

The second factor that could stall U.S.–Iranian cooperation is the prospect of an independent Kurdistan. Under Maliki, the relationship between Baghdad and the Kurdish regional capital of Erbil, became increasingly hostile. After the northern Iraqi city of Mosul fell to ISIS in June, the Kurds decided to seize the opportunity to make a bid for greater sovereignty. They quickly captured Kirkuk, a contested and energy-rich city in northern Iraq, and continued with their controversial policy to sell oil without Baghdad's approval. They also stated their intention to hold a referendum on Kurdish independence.

All of these developments alarmed Tehran, which has generally maintained good relations with the Kurds, but has drawn a red line regarding Kurdish independence. The recent decision by Western countries to provide weapons directly to Kurdish militias has increased Tehran's anxieties. Although Iran has developed close political and economic ties with Iraq's Kurds and has even pledged to support them in their war against ISIS, Tehran also understands that independence for Iraqi Kurds could easily incite Iran's own ethnic minorities to demand independence and undermine the country's territorial integrity. Tehran is very aware of a recent precedent: After World War II, an independent government was fleetingly established in Mahabad, in Iranian Kurdistan, although the Soviet-backed movement was soon crushed by Iran's central government. Iranian policymakers also know that, although the United States officially opposes Kurdish independence, the Kurds have powerful friends in Washington who seek to change that policy.

Finally, U.S.–Iranian cooperation can always falter because of the many constituencies in both countries that are ideologically opposed to any bilateral cooperation between the two states. In Washington, many blame Iran for encouraging sectarianism in Iraq, and correctly point out that Iran trained and funded the Shia militias that killed U.S. troops after the initial invasion of Iraq. They consider Iran to be the source of Iraq's problems and sincerely, if unrealistically, seek to exclude it from any future security architecture of the country. For example, General James L. Jones, Obama's former National Security Advisor, recently proposed convening a U.S.-sponsored strategic conference about Iraq. All regional players are to be invited to the conference, except Iran.

Similarly, many members of the security forces in Tehran reject cooperation with the United States. They believe that Washington is the source of instability in Iraq; some even blame the United States for the existence of ISIS, based on the conspiratorial belief that the United States helped finance the group so that it would fight against the Tehran-backed Assad regime in Syria. For Iran's most devout Islamist ideologues, the United States can never be trusted beyond very short-term tactical cooperation.

Despite these difficulties, cooperation between Washington and Tehran is likely to deepen, rather than ebb, in the weeks ahead. ISIS is a clear transnational threat that demands a transnational solution. Iran has considerable experience fighting against ISIS in Syria and Lebanon and can offer much assistance to those who seek to eradicate the threat posed by the militant group. Indeed, the fight against ISIS may even produce the previously unthinkable: cooperation between Iran and Saudi Arabia, two countries that have more or less fought an open proxy war for the past several years in Iraq, Lebanon, and Syria. Now, both countries are threatened by ISIS, which explains why Saudi Arabia openly welcomed Abadi's nomination to become prime minister.

Two weeks ago, Alaeddin Boroujerdi, chairman of the Iranian parliament's Foreign Policy and National Security Committee, correctly stated that Iran, Saudi Arabia, and the United States are the key players in Iraq. If Washington and Tehran manage to cooperate to stabilize in Iraq, it would not only be good news for the Iraqis—it could also pave the way for a final agreement in the ongoing nuclear negotiations. In that sense, the two countries would have truly achieved significant rapprochement, if not in the way that many observers originally anticipated.

They're Coming

Measuring the Threat from Returning Jihadists

Jytte Klausen OCTOBER 1, 2014

In an interview with the Washington Post in May, FBI Director James B. Comey, who also served as President George W. Bush's deputy attorney general, compared the wave of militants pouring into Syria and Iraq to the rush to join Osama bin Laden in Afghanistan as the Taliban swept that country. "We see Syria as that, but an order of magnitude worse in a couple of respects," he said. "Far more people going there. Far easier to travel to and back from."

But not everybody agrees that the United States should be alarmed. Writing in the New Yorker last month, the journalist Steve Coll pointed to "some terrorism specialists," who argue that Islamic State of Iraq and al-Sham (ISIS) is fighting a sectarian war and is more concerned with killing other Muslims than Westerners; that it "has shown no intent to launch attacks in the West, or any ability to do so." In a widely cited article in the American Political Science Review, Thomas Hegghammer, a senior research fellow at the Norwegian Defense Establishment, argued that there is an essential philosophical difference between those who carry out attacks at home and those who go abroad to fight on behalf of al Qaeda and its affiliates. Many of the Westerners who

JYTTE KLAUSEN is Lawrence A. Wien Professor of International Cooperation at Brandeis University.

have gone to Syria and Iraq, he wrote, are unlikely to want to attack targets at home.

Yet fighters returning from Syria have already attempted to carry out violent attacks in the West, and, in one instance, they succeeded. In October 2013, the London Metropolitan Police stopped a car traveling near the Tower of London carrying two men who were reportedly on their way to execute an attack. The two men, both London residents but not British citizens, had recently returned from Syria. In March this year, the French police unraveled a terrorist cell in Nice that was allegedly planning to use improvised explosive devices on the French Riviera. The perpetrators had also recently returned from Syria and were linked to a cell that was held responsible for an attack on a Paris kosher shop in September 2012. Then, at the end of May, Mehdi Nemmouche, a French citizen linked to a militant group known as Forsane Alizza (Knights of Pride), killed three people in front of the Jewish museum in Brussels. He also apparently took part in holding a group of journalists hostage in Syria between July 2013 and December 2013. In late July this year, the Norwegian government put the country on alert that four terrorists from ISIS were on their way to carry out a bombing in the country. The plan, it seems, was for the terrorists to kidnap a family, record themselves decapitating its members, and then post the video to YouTube. And finally, this week, the Australian police carried out the largest counterterrorism operation in the country's history against an ISIS-linked group based in Sydney. The group allegedly planned to carry out random beheadings of one or more pedestrians taken off the street.

BY THE NUMBERS

According to official estimates, about 3,000 Westerners have joined ISIS or Jabhat al-Nusra, the al Qaeda–affiliated group in Syria. In addition, hundreds of women from Europe and Australia (and a few Americans) have followed the men, marrying them online before they leave home or linking up with fighters after they arrive for training. They are already pushing against traditional jihadist gender boundaries by setting up female-only fighter groups and taking a prominent role on social media networks—including posting pictures of themselves with mutilated corpses. They could very well end up becoming violent themselves.

Here, historical data may provide a baseline estimate. For some years, I have worked with my students to track Westerners who have committed terrorist acts on behalf of al Qaeda and other jihadist groups in its mold. Between 2012 and May 2014, we identified—by name or fighter alias—600 who have left to fight in Syria and Iraq since June 2014. We also identified about 900 individuals who, between 1993 and until about 2012, fought in previous jihadist insurgencies or attempted to link up with terrorist groups and training camps abroad associated with al Qaeda, not including the jihadist groups in Syria and Iraq. Many of these veteran fighters fought in multiple insurgencies. Some of them are now back at work in Syria or Iraq, or have died fighting there. That makes for a data set of nearly 1,500 Western foreign fighters about whom we have basic demographic information, such as age and national and ethnic origin. We know which insurgency they participated in, and what they did after that.

The data show that, in fact, we should be very afraid of the "backflow" from Syria and Iraq. The experience of fighting in a foreign conflict zone, or receiving military-style training from a terrorist organization abroad, often primes Western militants to perpetrate a violent attack at home.

By our count, there have been approximately 279 violent terrorist plots on Western soil since 1993 that were unrelated to the ongoing mobilization in Syria and Iraq. (Here, "plot" might more accurately be described as an arrest related to plans or attempts to do something illegal related to terrorism.) Of the 279 plots, 114 (or 41 percent) included foreign fighters. We identified 275 foreign fighters overall who participated in these plots. Taking a baseline number of nearly 900 foreign fighters (all pre-Syria), in other words, approximately one-in-three Western fighters or veterans of training camps participated in a violent domestic plot. They also helped in fundraising, recruitment, and other schemes, but nonviolent activities are not included in this risk assessment.

Of course, producing clean metrics is tricky. "Doing something" abroad and at home are closely related events, and the sequence does not necessarily go "training abroad and then violent action at home." (Of the 275 identified participants, 235, about 85 percent, participated in a Western plot after returning.) On occasion, perpetrators became foreign fighters after attempting violence in the West. In those cases, they were often fleeing to join a terrorist group abroad to avoid presenting themselves in court for trial. Others launched attacks after going abroad and failing to obtain sponsorship from an al Qaeda affiliate. Tarek Mehanna, a pudgy pharmacy student from Sudbury, Massachusetts, made no less than three unsuccessful attempts to join an al Qaeda affiliate abroad. After one of his unsuccessful trips, he and his friends played with the idea of shooting up a local mall.

We can drill down still further to look at so-called homegrown conspiracies following 9/11 that have posed a significant risk of large-scale civilian casualties—for example, the Boston Marathon Bombings, the failed 2009 plot by three school friends from Queens to bomb the New York City subway, and Faisal Shahzad's failed 2010 Times Square car bomb. We identified 24 such extremely violent plots on Western soil. Of these, 79 percent—four out of five—involved returning foreign fighters or individuals who had received training abroad. Of all returning foreign fighters, about one in 12 attempted something along these lines.

In short, not all Westerners return home from jihad abroad to take part in a violent attack. But many do, and they tend to become involved with extremely dangerous plans. Of course, alarming as these numbers are, the ratio of disrupted violent incidents to actualized ones is high—about four-to-one—and has increased since the early years of homegrown terrorism following the 9/11 attacks. The odds of disruption for the plots that posed a significant risk of mass casualties are about 50–50.

ATTACK-READY

Assuming that past behavior contains some insights into future behavior, the historical data can help policymakers assess the risk posed to domestic safety by Western returnees from the battle in Syria and Iraq. Combat zone death rates are high among the Western volunteers in Syria and Iraq, about one-in-three, by our count. Generally, insurgent casualty rates are high, but the Westerners are also often used as suicide bombers. (As one former ISIS fighter put it: "I saw many foreign recruits who were put in the suicide squads not because they were 'great and God wanted it' as [ISIS] commanders praised them in front of us, but basically because they were useless for ISIS, they spoke no Arabic, they weren't good fighters and had no professional skills.") Accepting the estimate that there are (or have been) about 3,000 Western fighters in the theater, we would expect that about a thousand will die. Of those who don't, most return home or travel to another Western country. Using the one-in-three ratio of returnees from previous conflicts who have come back to do something violent, we would expect over 600 returning fighters from Syria and Iraq to attempt to carry out a violent attack in a Western country within the next few years. This number does not include the essentially unknowable risk stemming from the women who have become radicalized during the time spent with their husbands in Iraq and Syria.

This is not to say that the current wave of jihadists is the same as previous waves. First, the demographics of Westerners in Syria and Iraq today are very different from those in previous jihadist insurgencies. For one, Western fighters in Syria are generally younger (with a mean age of 24) than in previous conflicts. In Bosnia, the average age was 30. In Pakistan and Afghanistan, before and after 9/11, the average was around 27. In the first jihadist insurgency in Iraq (2004–07), the fighters were nearly 28 years old. Recruitment through social media is often held responsible for the age shift, but ISIS has also deliberately recruited very young fighters, even teenagers. Further, the fighters in Syria and Iraq are far more diverse in terms of ancestral origin and race, with white

Europeans comprising about 20 percent. No clear socio-economic profile exists either, with gang members from Europe's ethnic enclaves and drop-outs from universities and prestigious private schools joining up in equal measure. And, finally, there are more women because of militant groups' policy of getting young jihadists married very early. Some of these factors would seem to indicate a heightened risk—for example, the increased involvement of women would arguably expand the pool of possible attackers. Other factors are more ambiguous—young people on a jihadist "gap year" may return home regretting what they have done. Or they might want to go elsewhere and do something more when, if they survive, they leave or are expelled from Iraq and Syria.

Second, unlike before 9/11, when recruitment was a product of direct contact with exiled preachers based in the West, today, the recruitment of Westerners to fight in Syria and Iraq comes from extensive jihadist organizations in the West with deep roots and long histories of perpetrating violent attacks. The fighters in Syria and Iraq are thus deeply enmeshed in networks that were already responsible for violent incidents in West before the Syrian conflict captured their attention. That will increase the likelihood that returnees will be redirected to plots in the West or dispatched to other insurgencies abroad.

Finally, the jihadist ideology has changed from previous conflicts. In Afghanistan, the enemy was the Soviet Union. In Bosnia, it was the Serbs. In Somalia, it was the Ethiopians. In Syria and Iraq, the fight is primarily against other Muslims. And the jihadist insurgents in Syria and Iraq —irrespective of their factional differences—share a strategic interest in expanding the conflict to the whole of the Middle East so that they can undo the much-hated Sykes–Picot borders that effectively divided the collapsing Ottoman Empire into British and French protectorates. These terrorists recognize no borders or territorial limits to their fight. And that, too, increases the risk that the returnees may become a significant security risk at home.

Jytte Klausen

OUNCE OF PREVENTION

So what can the West do? Above all, it cannot discount the threat of Western fighters in foreign conflicts. There are simply too many, and their ability and willingness to launch major attacks on the West is too great, to ignore.

Preventing people from leaving to fight with a terrorist organization in the first place is an urgent priority. All, or nearly all, of the newly minted Western-based jihadists from the Syrian and Iraqi conflicts hold Western passports. Current administrative controls target suspected terrorists and individuals who are known to have committed terrorist acts but who, for one reason or another, cannot be charged with criminal offenses. Measures range from impounding passports to imposing house arrests and curfews on individuals who are considered a risk to public safety.

To tackle the migration of a growing number of Western citizens to the frontlines of terrorist campaigns, though, preventive restrictions would have to be extended to hundreds if not thousands of people. Governments are already impounding passports in bulk, but ad hoc measures imposed in the absence of public debate will spawn a backlash against counterterrorism efforts down the road. Restricting the rights of citizens to travel is contrary to core Western values and, within the European Union, runs counter to years of efforts to promote mobility.

In the meantime, the West will have to calibrate its policing strategies to allow non-combatants and those with regrets to come home, while sorting out dangerous individuals for prosecution and detention. For pragmatic reasons—ranging from problems with obtaining evidence that meets the exacting standards of war crimes prosecutions to cost considerations—the authorities are likely to opt for prosecutions on lesser charges for which the evidence may be obtained closer to home. That is, they might focus on crimes committed in the West during the preparation for terrorist acts committed abroad. On the positive side, such a strategy could get dangerous terrorists off the street. On the negative, it will bring little comfort to the victims in Iraq and Syria, and Western states may look unwilling to punish their own citizens for crimes against non-Westerners.

A strategy for rehabilitation of post-conflict returnees who cannot be charged with criminal offenses is a must. As the conflict intensifies and casualties grow in Syria and Iraq, many of the less-experienced fighters, the teenagers and the women, will want to come home. Some will be traumatized. A few may even express regrets. Good counter-radicalization and rehabilitation strategies draw on the experience of dealing with gangs: Teams of law enforcement agents and social workers collaborate to provide mentors to former members. They also implement various types of direct supervision—bans on access to computers, for example, and limitations on the right to communicate with particular individuals. An advantage of the rehabilitation approach is that local authorities are able to keep a close watch on specific individuals and involve families.

Finally, there is the matter of providing justice to the victims. Westerners have participated in executions and crucifixions and raped and plundered in Syria and Iraq. Anticipating war crimes prosecutions of returnees, a number of countries (Sweden, France, Spain, and Canada) have recently enshrined crimes against humanity in their own countries' penal code, allowing domestic courts to prosecute severe crimes committed abroad. But such prosecutions require custody of the accused.

In other words, bringing the most hardened Western foreign fighters to justice would require their capture and rendition on a large scale. No precedent exists for legal renditions and judicial cooperation of this scale. In the past, European courts have spent years fighting over extraditions of terrorists wanted for trial elsewhere. Khaled al-Fawwaz, bin Laden's secretary, went about his business in London for more than a decade before he was extradited to stand trial in the United States on charges in connection with his role in the planning of the 1998 bombings of the U.S. embassies in Kenya and Tanzania. (The trial is set for November 3 in the Southern District of New York.)

Jytte Klausen

The West is now faced with a foreign fighter problem of an unprecedented scale. It can expect that Westerners currently in Iraq and Syria will continue to commit atrocities abroad and will come home and attempt some kind of terrorist plot. It can expect most of the plots on Western soil to be thwarted and the perpetrators rounded up. That means, however, that the Western legal systems will have to finally adjust to dealing with unprecedented numbers of very dangerous people committing crimes for which the evidence is largely foreign, photographic, or found online. The risk of not doing so is already evident: a decade of terrorist recruitment in the West that drew thousands of young people into a violent revolutionary movement—all without provoking much of a response.

In the United States, the panic that Americans will soon be slaughtered in their beds by returning jihadists is barely concealed. That will not happen, but a realistic assessment of the scale of the threat nonetheless calls for extraordinary measures and international collaboration on the prevention, discovery, apprehension, and detention of the operatives that are responsible for funneling Western recruits into jihad campaigns abroad.

Welcome to the Revolution

Why Shale Is the Next Shale

Edward L. Morse   FROM OUR MAY/JUNE 2014 ISSUE

Despite its doubters and haters, the shale revolution in oil and gas production is here to stay. In the second half of this decade, moreover, it is likely to spread globally more quickly than most think. And all of that is, on balance, a good thing for the world.

The recent surge of U.S. oil and natural gas production has been nothing short of astonishing. For the past three years, the United States has been the world's fastest-growing hydrocarbon producer, and the trend is not likely to stop anytime soon. U.S. natural gas production has risen by 25 percent since 2010, and the only reason it has temporarily stalled is that investments are required to facilitate further growth. Having already outstripped Russia as the world's largest gas producer, by the end of the decade, the United States will become one of the world's largest gas exporters, fundamentally changing pricing and trade patterns in global energy markets. U.S. oil production, meanwhile, has grown by 60 percent since 2008, climbing by three million barrels a day to more than eight million barrels a day. Within a couple of years, it will exceed its old record level of almost ten million barrels a day as the United States overtakes Russia and Saudi Arabia and becomes the world's largest oil producer. And U.S. production of

EDWARD L. MORSE is Global Head of Commodities Research at Citi.

natural gas liquids, such as propane and butane, has already grown by one million barrels per day and should grow by another million soon.

What is unfolding in reaction is nothing less than a paradigm shift in thinking about hydrocarbons. A decade ago, there was a near-global consensus that U.S. (and, for that matter, non-OPEC) production was in inexorable decline. Today, most serious analysts are confident that it will continue to grow. The growth is occurring, to boot, at a time when U.S. oil consumption is falling. (Forget peak oil production; given a combination of efficiency gains, environmental concerns, and substitution by natural gas, what is foreseeable is peak oil demand.) And to cap things off, the costs of finding and producing oil and gas in shale and tight rock formations are steadily going down and will drop even more in the years to come.

The evidence from what has been happening is now overwhelming. Efficiency gains in the shale sector have been large and accelerating and are now hovering at around 25 percent per year, meaning that increases in capital expenditures are triggering even more potential production growth. It is clear that vast amounts of hydrocarbons have migrated from their original source rock and become trapped in shale and tight rock, and the extent of these rock formations, like the extent of the original source rock, is enormous—containing resources far in excess of total global conventional proven oil reserves, which are 1.5 trillion barrels. And there are already signs that the technology involved in extracting these resources is transferable outside the United States, so that its international spread is inevitable.

In short, it now looks as though the first few decades of the twenty-first century will see an extension of the trend that has persisted for the past few millennia: the availability of plentiful energy at ever-lower cost and with ever-greater efficiency, enabling major advances in global economic growth.

WHY THE PAST IS PROLOGUE

The shale revolution has been very much a "made in America" phenomenon. In no other country can landowners also own mineral rights. In only a few other countries (such as Australia, Canada, and the United Kingdom) is there a tradition of an energy sector featuring many independent entrepreneurial companies, as opposed to a few major companies or national champions. And in still fewer countries are there capital markets able and willing to support financially risky exploration and production.

This powerful combination of indigenous factors will continue to drive U.S. efforts. A further 30 percent increase in U.S. natural gas production is plausible before 2020, and from then on, it should be possible to maintain a constant or even higher level of production for decades to come. As for oil, given the research and development now under way, it is likely that U.S. production could rise to 12 million barrels per day or more in a few years and be sustained there for a long time. (And that figure does not include additional potential output from deep-water drilling, which is also seeing a renaissance in investment.)

Two factors, meanwhile, should bring prices down for a long time to come. The first is declining production costs, a consequence of efficiency gains from the application of new and growing technologies. And the second is the spread of shale gas and tight oil production globally. Together, these suggest a sustainable price of around $5.50 per thousand cubic feet for natural gas in the United States and a trading range of $70–$90 per barrel for oil globally by the end of this decade.

These trends will provide a significant boost to the U.S. economy. Households could save close to $30 billion annually in electricity costs by 2020, compared to the U.S. Energy Information Administration's current forecast. Gasoline costs could fall from an average of five percent to three percent of real disposable personal income. The price of gasoline could drop by 30 percent, increasing annual disposable income by $750, on average, per driving household. The oil and gas boom could add about 2.8 percent in cumulative GDP growth by 2020 and bolster employment by some three million jobs.

Beyond the United States, the spread of shale gas and tight oil exploitation should have geopolitically profound implications. There is no longer any doubt about the sheer abundance of this new accessible resource base, and that recognition is leading many governments to accelerate the delineation and development of commercially available resources. Countries' motivations are diverse and clear. For Saudi Arabia, which is already developing its first power plant using indigenous shale gas, the exploitation of its shale resources can free up more oil for exports, increasing revenues for the country as a whole. For Russia, with an estimated 75 billion barrels of recoverable tight oil (50 percent more than the United States), production growth spells more government revenue. And for a host of other countries, the motivations range from reducing dependence on imports to increasing export earnings to enabling domestic economic development.

RISKY BUSINESS?

Skeptics point to three problems that could lead the fruits of the revolution to be left to wither on the vine: environmental regulation, declining rates of production, and drilling economics. But none is likely to be catastrophic.

Hydraulic fracturing, or "fracking"—the process of injecting sand, water, and chemicals into shale rocks to crack them open and release the hydrocarbons trapped inside—poses potential environmental risks, such as the draining or polluting of underground aquifers, the spurring of seismic activity, and the spilling of waste products during their aboveground transport. All these risks can be mitigated, and they are in fact being addressed in the industry's evolving set of best practices. But that message needs to be delivered more clearly, and best practices need to be implemented across the board, in order to head off local bans or restrictive regulation that would slow the revolution's spread or minimize its impact.

As for declining rates of production, fracking creates a surge in production at the beginning of a well's operation and a rapid drop later on, and critics argue that this means that the revolution's purported gains will be illusory. But there are two good reasons to think that high production will continue for decades rather than years. First, the accumulation of fracked wells with a long tail of production is building up a durable base of flows that will continue over time, and second, the economics of drilling work in favor of drilling at a high and sustained rate of production.

Finally, some criticize the economics of fracking, but these concerns have been exaggerated. It is true that through 2013, the upstream sector of the U.S. oil and gas industry has been massively cash-flow negative. In 2012, for example, the industry spent about $60 billion more than it earned, and some analysts believe that such trends will continue. But the costs were driven by the need to acquire land for exploration and to pursue unproductive drilling in order to hold the acreage. Now that the land-grab days are almost over, the industry's cash flow should be increasingly positive.

It is also true that traditional finding and development costs indicate that natural gas prices need to be above $4 per thousand cubic feet and oil prices above $70 per barrel for the economics of drilling to work—which suggests that abundant production might drive prices down below what is profitable. But as demand grows for natural gas—for industry, residential and commercial space heating, the export market, power generation, and transportation—prices should rise to a level that can sustain increased drilling: the $5–$6 range, which is about where prices were this past winter. Efficiency gains stemming from new technology, meanwhile, are driving down break-even drilling costs. In the oil sector, most drilling now brings an adequate return on investment at prices below $50 per barrel, and within a few years, that level could be under $40 per barrel.

Edward L. Morse

THINK GLOBALLY

Since shale resources are found around the globe, many countries are trying to duplicate the United States' success in the sector, and it is likely that some, and perhaps many, will succeed. U.S. recoverable shale resources constitute only about 15 percent of the global total, and so if the true extent and duration of even the U.S. windfall are not yet measurable, the same applies even more so for the rest of the world. Many countries are already taking early steps to develop their shale resources, and in several, the results look promising. It is highly likely that Australia, China, Mexico, Russia, Saudi Arabia, and the United Kingdom will see meaningful production before the end of this decade. As a result, global trade in energy will be dramatically disrupted.

A few years ago, hydrocarbon exports from the United States were negligible. But by the start of 2013, oil, natural gas, and petrochemicals had become the single largest category of U.S. exports, surpassing agricultural products, transportation equipment, and capital goods. The shift in the U.S. trade balance for petroleum products has been stunning. In 2008, the United States was a net importer of petroleum products, taking in about two million barrels per day; by the end of 2013, it was a net exporter, with an outflow of more than two million barrels per day. By the end of 2014, the United States should overtake Russia as the largest exporter of diesel, jet fuel, and other energy products, and by 2015, it should overtake Saudi Arabia as the largest exporter of petrochemical feedstocks. The U.S. trade balance for oil, which in 2011 was –$354 billion, should flip to +$5 billion by 2020.

By then, the United States will be a net exporter of natural gas, on a scale potentially rivaling both Qatar and Russia, and the consequences will be enormous. The U.S. gas trade balance should shift from –$8 billion in 2013 to +$14 billion by 2020. U.S. pipeline exports to Mexico and eastern Canada are likely to grow by 400 percent, to eight billion cubic feet per day, by 2018, and perhaps to ten billion by 2020. U.S. exports of liquefied natural gas (LNG) look likely to reach nine billion cubic feet per day by 2020.

Sheer volume is important, but not as much as two other factors: the pricing basis and the amount of natural gas that can be sold in a spot market. Most LNG trade links the price of natural gas to the price of oil. But the shale gas revolution has delinked these two prices in the United States, where the traditional 7:1 ratio between oil and gas prices has exploded to more than 20:1. That makes LNG exports from the United States competitive with LNG exports from Qatar or Russia, eroding the oil link in LNG pricing. What's more, traditional LNG contracts are tied to specific destinations and prohibit trading. U.S. LNG (and likely also new LNG from Australia and Canada) will not come with anticompetitive trade restrictions, and so a spot market should emerge quickly. And U.S. LNG exports to Europe should erode the Russian state oil company Gazprom's pricing hold on the continent, just as they should bring down prices of natural gas around the world.

In the geopolitics of energy, there are always winners and losers. OPEC will be among the latter, as the United States moves from having had a net hydrocarbon trade deficit of some nine million barrels per day in 2007, to having one of under six million barrels today, to enjoying a net positive position by 2020. Lost market share and lower prices could pose a devastating challenge to oil producers dependent on exports for government revenue. Growing populations and declining per capita incomes are already playing a central role in triggering domestic upheaval in Iraq, Libya, Nigeria, and Venezuela, and in that regard, the years ahead do not look promising for those countries.

At the same time, the U.S. economy might actually start approaching energy independence. And the shale revolution should also lead to the prevalence of market forces in international energy pricing, putting an end to OPEC's 40-year dominance, during which producers were able to band together to raise prices well above production costs, with negative consequences for the world economy. When it comes to oil and natural gas, we now know that though much is taken, much abides—and the shale revolution is only just getting started.

New World Order

Labor, Capital, and Ideas in the Power Law Economy

Erik Brynjolfsson, Andrew McAfee, and Michael Spence

FROM OUR JULY/
AUGUST 2014 ISSUE

R ecent advances in technology have created an increasingly unified global marketplace for labor and capital. The ability of both to flow to their highest-value uses, regardless of their location, is equalizing their prices across the globe. In recent years, this broad factor-price equalization has benefited nations with abundant low-cost labor and those with access to cheap capital. Some have argued that the current era of rapid technological progress serves labor, and some have argued that it serves capital. What both camps have slighted is the fact that technology is not only integrating existing sources of labor and capital but also creating new ones.

Machines are substituting for more types of human labor than ever before. As they replicate themselves, they are also creating more capital. This means that the real winners of the future will

ERIK BRYNJOLFSSON is Schussel Family Professor of Management Science at the MIT Sloan School of Management and Co-Founder of MIT's Initiative on the Digital Economy.

ANDREW MCAFEE is a Principal Research Scientist at the MIT Center for Digital Business at the MIT Sloan School of Management and Co-Founder of MIT's Initiative on the Digital Economy.

MICHAEL SPENCE is William R. Berkley Professor in Economics and Business at the NYU Stern School of Business.

not be the providers of cheap labor or the owners of ordinary capital, both of whom will be increasingly squeezed by automation. Fortune will instead favor a third group: those who can innovate and create new products, services, and business models.

The distribution of income for this creative class typically takes the form of a power law, with a small number of winners capturing most of the rewards and a long tail consisting of the rest of the participants. So in the future, ideas will be the real scarce inputs in the world—scarcer than both labor and capital—and the few who provide good ideas will reap huge rewards. Assuring an acceptable standard of living for the rest and building inclusive economies and societies will become increasingly important challenges in the years to come.

LABOR PAINS

In the future, ideas will be the real scarce inputs—scarcer than both labor and capital.

Turn over your iPhone and you can read an eight-word business plan that has served Apple well: "Designed by Apple in California. Assembled in China." With a market capitalization of over $500 billion, Apple has become the most valuable company in the world. Variants of this strategy have worked not only for Apple and other large global enterprises but also for medium-sized firms and even "micro-multinationals." More and more companies have been riding the two great forces of our era—technology and globalization—to profits.

Technology has sped globalization forward, dramatically lowering communication and transaction costs and moving the world much closer to a single, large global market for labor, capital, and other inputs to production. Even though labor is not fully mobile, the other factors increasingly are. As a result, the various components of global supply chains can move to labor's location with little friction or cost. About one-third of the goods and services in advanced economies are tradable, and the figure is rising. And the effect of global competition spills over to the nontradable part of the economy, in both advanced and developing economies.

All of this creates opportunities for not only greater efficiencies and profits but also enormous dislocations. If a worker in China or India can do the same work as one in the United States, then the laws of economics dictate that they will end up earning similar wages (adjusted for some other differences in national productivity). That's good news for overall economic efficiency, for consumers, and for workers in developing countries—but not for workers in developed countries who now face low-cost competition. Research indicates that the tradable sectors of advanced industrial countries have not been net employment generators for two decades. That means job creation now takes place almost exclusively within the large nontradable sector, whose wages are held down by increasing competition from workers displaced from the tradable sector.

Even as the globalization story continues, however, an even bigger one is starting to unfold: the story of automation, including artificial intelligence, robotics, 3-D printing, and so on. And this second story is surpassing the first, with some of its greatest effects destined to hit relatively unskilled workers in developing nations.

Visit a factory in China's Guangdong Province, for example, and you will see thousands of young people working day in and day out on routine, repetitive tasks, such as connecting two parts of a keyboard. Such jobs are rarely, if ever, seen anymore in the United States or the rest of the rich world. But they may not exist for long in China and the rest of the developing world either, for they involve exactly the type of tasks that are easy for robots to do. As intelligent machines become cheaper and more capable, they will increasingly replace human labor, especially in relatively structured environments such as factories and especially for the most routine and repetitive tasks. To put it another way, offshoring is often only a way station on the road to automation.

This will happen even where labor costs are low. Indeed, Foxconn, the Chinese company that assembles iPhones and iPads, employs more than a million low-income workers—but now, it is supplementing and replacing them with a growing army of robots.

So after many manufacturing jobs moved from the United States to China, they appear to be vanishing from China as well. (Reliable data on this transition are hard to come by. Official Chinese figures report a decline of 30 million manufacturing jobs since 1996, or 25 percent of the total, even as manufacturing output has soared by over 70 percent, but part of that drop may reflect revisions in the methods of gathering data.) As work stops chasing cheap labor, moreover, it will gravitate toward wherever the final market is, since that will add value by shortening delivery times, reducing inventory costs, and the like.

The growing capabilities of automation threaten one of the most reliable strategies that poor countries have used to attract outside investment: offering low wages to compensate for low productivity and skill levels. And the trend will extend beyond manufacturing. Interactive voice response systems, for example, are reducing the requirement for direct person-to-person interaction, spelling trouble for call centers in the developing world. Similarly, increasingly reliable computer programs will cut into transcription work now often done in the developing world. In more and more domains, the most cost-effective source of "labor" is becoming intelligent and flexible machines as opposed to low-wage humans in other countries.

CAPITAL PUNISHMENT

If cheap, abundant labor is no longer a clear path to economic progress, then what is? One school of thought points to the growing contributions of capital: the physical and intangible assets that combine with labor to produce the goods and services in an economy (think of equipment, buildings, patents, brands, and so on). As the economist Thomas Piketty argues in his best-selling book *Capital in the Twenty-first Century*, capital's share of the economy tends to grow when the rate of return on it is greater than the general rate of economic growth, a condition he predicts for the future. The "capital deepening" of economies that Piketty forecasts will be accelerated further as robots, computers, and software (all of which are forms of capital) increasingly substitute for human workers. Evidence indicates that just such a form of capital-based technological change is taking place in the United States and around the world.

In the past decade, the historically consistent division in the United States between the share of total national income going to labor and that going to physical capital seems to have changed significantly. As the economists Susan Fleck, John Glaser, and Shawn Sprague noted in the U.S. Bureau of Labor Statistics' *Monthly Labor Review* in 2011, "Labor share averaged 64.3 percent from 1947 to 2000. Labor share has declined over the past decade, falling to its lowest point in the third quarter of 2010, 57.8 percent." Recent moves to "re-shore" production from overseas, including Apple's decision to produce its new Mac Pro computer in Texas, will do little to reverse this trend. For in order to be economically viable, these new domestic manufacturing facilities will need to be highly automated.

Other countries are witnessing similar trends. The economists Loukas Karabarbounis and Brent Neiman have documented significant declines in labor's share of GDP in 42 of the 59 countries they studied, including China, India, and Mexico. In describing their findings, Karabarbounis and Neiman are explicit that progress in digital technologies is an important driver of this phenomenon: "The decrease in the relative price of investment goods, often attributed to advances in information technology and the computer age, induced firms to shift away from labor and toward capital. The lower price of investment goods explains roughly half of the observed decline in the labor share."

But if capital's share of national income has been growing, the continuation of such a trend into the future may be in jeopardy as a new challenge to capital emerges—not from a revived labor sector but from an increasingly important unit within its own ranks: digital capital.

In a free market, the biggest premiums go to the scarcest inputs needed for production. In a world where capital such as software and robots can be replicated cheaply, its marginal value will tend to fall, even if more of it is used in the aggregate. And as more capital is added cheaply at the margin, the value of existing capital will actually be driven down. Unlike, say, traditional factories, many types of digital capital can be added extremely cheaply. Software can be duplicated and distributed at almost zero incremental cost. And many elements of computer hardware, governed by variants of Moore's law, get quickly and consistently cheaper over time. Digital capital, in short, is abundant, has low marginal costs, and is increasingly important in almost every industry.

Even as production becomes more capital-intensive, therefore, the rewards earned by capitalists as a group may not necessarily continue to grow relative to labor. The shares will depend on the exact details of the production, distribution, and governance systems.

Most of all, the payoff will depend on which inputs to production are scarcest. If digital technologies create cheap substitutes for a growing set of jobs, then it is not a good time to be a laborer. But if digital technologies also increasingly substitute for capital, then all owners of capital should not expect to earn outsized returns, either.

TECHCRUNCH DISRUPT

What will be the scarcest, and hence the most valuable, resource in what two of us (Erik Brynjolfsson and Andrew McAfee) have called "the second machine age," an era driven by digital technologies and their associated economic characteristics? It will be neither ordinary labor nor ordinary capital but people who can create new ideas and innovations.

Such people have always been economically valuable, of course, and have often profited handsomely from their innovations as a result. But they had to share the returns on their ideas with the labor and capital that were necessary for bringing them into the marketplace. Digital technologies increasingly make both ordinary labor and ordinary capital commodities, and so a greater share of the rewards from ideas will go to the creators, innovators, and entrepreneurs. People with ideas, not workers or investors, will be the scarcest resource.

The most basic model economists use to explain technology's impact treats it as a simple multiplier for everything else, increasing overall productivity evenly for everyone. This model is used in most introductory economics classes and provides the foundation for the common—and, until recently, very sensible—intuition that a rising tide of technological progress will lift all boats equally, making all workers more productive and hence more valuable.

A slightly more complex and realistic model, however, allows for the possibility that technology may not affect all inputs equally but instead favor some more than others. Skill-based technical change, for example, plays to the advantage of more skilled workers relative to less skilled ones, and capital-based technical change favors capital relative to labor. Both of those types of technical change have been important in the past, but increasingly, a third type—what we call superstar-based technical change—is upending the global economy.

Today, it is possible to take many important goods, services, and processes and codify them. Once codified, they can be digitized, and once digitized, they can be replicated. Digital copies can be made at virtually zero cost and transmitted anywhere in the world almost instantaneously, each an exact replica of the original. The combination of these three characteristics—extremely low cost, rapid ubiquity, and perfect fidelity—leads to some weird and wonderful economics. It can create abundance where there had been scarcity, not only for consumer goods, such as music videos, but also for economic inputs, such as certain types of labor and capital.

The returns in such markets typically follow a distinct pattern—a power law, or Pareto curve, in which a small number of players reap a disproportionate share of the rewards. Network effects, whereby a product becomes more valuable the more users it has, can also generate these kinds of winner-take-all or winner-take-most markets. Consider Instagram, the photo-sharing platform, as an example of the economics of the digital, networked economy. The 14 people who created the company didn't need a lot of unskilled human helpers to do so, nor did they need much physical capital. They built a digital product that benefited from network effects, and when it caught on quickly, they were able to sell it after only a year and a half for nearly three-quarters of a billion dollars—ironically, months after the bankruptcy of another photography company, Kodak, that at its peak had employed some 145,000 people and held billions of dollars in capital assets.

Instagram is an extreme example of a more general rule. More often than not, when improvements in digital technologies make it more attractive to digitize a product or process, superstars see a boost in their incomes, whereas second bests, second movers, and latecomers have a harder time competing. The top performers in music, sports, and other areas have also seen their reach and incomes grow since the 1980s, directly or indirectly riding the same trends upward.

But it is not only software and media that are being transformed. Digitization and networks are becoming more pervasive in every industry and function across the economy, from retail and financial services to manufacturing and marketing. That means superstar economics are affecting more goods, services, and people than ever before.

Even top executives have started earning rock-star compensation. In 1990, CEO pay in the United States was, on average, 70 times as large as the salaries of other workers; in 2005, it was 300 times as large. Executive compensation more generally has been going in the same direction globally, albeit with considerable variation from country to country. Many forces are at work here, including tax and policy changes, evolving cultural and organizational norms, and plain luck. But as research by one of us (Brynjolfsson) and Heekyung Kim has shown, a portion of the growth is linked to the greater use of information technology. Technology expands the potential reach, scale, and monitoring capacity of a decision-maker, increasing the value of a good decision-maker by magnifying the potential consequences of his or her choices. Direct management via digital technologies makes a good manager more valuable than in earlier times, when executives had to share control with long chains of subordinates and could affect only a smaller range of activities. Today, the larger the market value of a company, the more compelling the argument for trying to get the very best executives to lead it.

When income is distributed according to a power law, most people will be below the average, and as national economies writ large are increasingly subject to such dynamics, that pattern will play itself out on the national level. And sure enough, the United States today features one of the world's highest levels of real GDP per capita—even as its median income has essentially stagnated for two decades.

PREPARING FOR THE PERMANENT REVOLUTION

The forces at work in the second machine age are powerful, interactive, and complex. It is impossible to look far into the future and predict with any precision what their ultimate impact will be. If individuals, businesses, and governments understand what is going on, however, they can at least try to adjust and adapt.

The United States, for example, stands to win back some business as the second sentence of Apple's eight-word business plan is overturned because its technology and manufacturing operations are once again performed inside U.S. borders. But the first sentence of the plan will become more important than ever, and here, concern, rather than complacency, is in order. For unfortunately, the dynamism and creativity that have made the United States the most innovative nation in the world may be faltering.

Thanks to the ever-onrushing digital revolution, design and innovation have now become part of the tradable sector of the global economy and will face the same sort of competition that has already transformed manufacturing. Leadership in design depends on an educated work force and an entrepreneurial culture, and the traditional American advantage in these areas is declining. Although the United States once led the world in the share of graduates in the work force with at least an associate's degree, it has now fallen to 12th place. And despite the buzz about entrepreneurship in places such as Silicon Valley, data show that since 1996, the number of U.S. start-ups employing more than one person has declined by over 20 percent.

If the trends under discussion are global, their local effects will be shaped, in part, by the social policies and investments that countries choose to make, both in the education sector specifically and in fostering innovation and economic dynamism more generally. For over a century, the U.S. educational system was the envy of the world, with universal K–12 schooling and world-class universities propelling sustained economic growth. But in recent decades, U.S. primary and secondary schooling have become increasingly uneven, with their quality based on neighborhood income levels and often a continued emphasis on rote learning.

Fortunately, the same digital revolution that is transforming product and labor markets can help transform education as well. Online learning can provide students with access to the best teachers, content, and methods regardless of their location, and new data-driven approaches to the field can make it easier to measure students' strengths, weaknesses, and progress. This should create opportunities for personalized learning programs and continuous improvement, using some of the feedback techniques that have already transformed scientific discovery, retail, and manufacturing.

Globalization and technological change may increase the wealth and economic efficiency of nations and the world at large, but they will not work to everybody's advantage, at least in the short to medium term. Ordinary workers, in particular, will continue to bear the brunt of the changes, benefiting as consumers but not necessarily as producers. This means that without further intervention, economic inequality is likely to continue to increase, posing a variety of problems. Unequal incomes can lead to unequal opportunities, depriving nations of access to talent and undermining the social contract. Political power, meanwhile, often follows economic power, in this case undermining democracy.

These challenges can and need to be addressed through the public provision of high-quality basic services, including education, health care, and retirement security. Such services will be crucial for creating genuine equality of opportunity in a rapidly changing economic environment and increasing intergenerational mobility in income, wealth, and future prospects.

As for spurring economic growth in general, there is a near consensus among serious economists about many of the policies that are necessary. The basic strategy is intellectually simple, if politically difficult: boost public-sector investment over the short and medium term while making such investment more efficient and putting in place a fiscal consolidation plan over the longer term. Public investments are known to yield high returns in basic research in health, science, and technology; in education; and in infrastructure spending on roads, airports, public water and sanitation systems, and energy and communications grids. Increased government spending in these areas would boost economic growth now even as it created real wealth for subsequent generations later.

Should the digital revolution continue to be as powerful in the future as it has been in recent years, the structure of the modern economy and the role of work itself may need to be rethought. As a group, our descendants may work fewer hours and live better—but both the work and the rewards could be spread even more unequally, with a variety of unpleasant consequences. Creating sustainable, equitable, and inclusive growth will require more than business as usual. The place to start is with a proper understanding of just how fast and far things are evolving.

The Strategic Logic of Trade

New Rules of the Road for the Global Market

Michael B. Froman

FROM OUR NOVEMBER/
DECEMBER 2014 ISSUE

For much of the twentieth century, leaders and policymakers around the world viewed the strategic importance of trade, and of international economic policy more generally, largely through the lens of military strength. They believed that the role of a strong economy was to act as an enabler, supporting a strong military, which they saw as the best way to project power and influence. But in recent decades, leaders have come to see the economic clout that trade produces as more than merely a purse for military prowess: they now understand prosperity to be a principal means by which countries measure and exercise power.

The strategic importance of trade is not new, but it has grown in recent years and strongly reinforces the economic case for expanding trade. Over 40 years ago, the economist Thomas Schelling observed, "Broadly defined to include investment, shipping, tourism, and the management of enterprises, trade is what most of international relations are about. For that reason trade policy is national security policy." In a world where markets can have as much influence as militaries, any tension between the United States' national security priorities and its economic goals is more apparent than

MICHAEL FROMAN is the U.S. Trade Representative.

real. Still, in considering new trade agreements, Washington must first and foremost evaluate their economic merits. Trade deals must promote U.S. economic growth, support jobs, and strengthen the middle class.

Trade's contribution to the U.S. economy has never been more significant than it is today. Trade supports higher-paying jobs, spurs economic growth, and enhances the competitiveness of the U.S. economy. Last year, the United States exported a record $2.3 trillion in goods and services, which in turn supported around 11.3 million American jobs. Over the last five years, the increase in U.S. exports has accounted for nearly a third of total U.S. economic growth and, during the past four years, has supported 1.6 million additional jobs. Better yet, those jobs typically pay somewhere between 13 and 18 percent more than jobs unrelated to exports.

Moreover, trade plays a major role in attracting investors and manufacturers to the United States. The country offers a massive market, strong rule of law, a skilled work force with an entrepreneurial culture, and increasingly abundant sources of affordable energy. The Obama administration's trade policy seeks to make the United States even more attractive to investors by positioning the country at the center of a web of agreements that will provide unfettered access to nearly two-thirds of the global economy. As a result, the United States is already enjoying increased investment, attracting manufacturing jobs, and establishing itself as the world's production platform of choice. Companies of all sizes once again want to make things in the United States and export them all over the world.

The United States can compete in the global marketplace and win—if the playing field is level.

For nearly seven decades, the global trading system has accomplished the goals of its lead architects, including U.S. statesmen such as Dean Acheson and George Marshall. It has brought jobs to American shores and peace and prosperity to countries around the world. But no one should take that system for granted. In recent years, tectonic shifts, such as economic globalization, technological change, and the rise of emerging economies, have reshaped the international landscape. As President Barack Obama remarked earlier this year, "Just as the world has changed, this architecture must change as well."

To help achieve that change, the Obama administration's trade agenda focuses on three strategic objectives: establishing and enforcing rules of the road, strengthening U.S. partnerships with other countries, and spurring broad-based economic development. Each of these objectives serves the overarching goals of revitalizing the global trading system, allowing the United States to continue to play a leading role in it, and ensuring that it reflects both American interests and American values.

RULES OF THE ROAD

With some of the most innovative companies and productive workers in the world, the United States can compete in the global marketplace and win—if the playing field is level. The Obama administration has made enforcement of the rules governing trade a top priority, and every time the administration has brought a dispute before the World Trade Organization and the WTO has made a decision, the United States has won. Preventing China from restricting access to rare-earth minerals and stopping Argentina from wrongly restricting imports of agricultural products—to cite just two examples—not only benefits U.S. workers, farmers, and businesses but also reinforces the rules-based trading system itself.

The Trans-Pacific Partnership presents an unprecedented opportunity to update the rules of the road. An ambitious and comprehensive trade agreement that the United States is currently negotiating with 11 countries in the Asia-Pacific region, the TPP represents a main pillar of the Obama administration's broader strategy of rebalancing toward Asia. Taken together, the parties negotiating the TPP represent nearly 40 percent of the world's GDP and account for roughly a third of all global trade.

This agreement would level the playing field of international trade by establishing the strongest environmental and labor standards of any trade agreement in U.S. history. For example, the United States is pressing other countries to address forced labor and child labor and to maintain acceptable working conditions. The United States has also broken new ground with proposals that would address illicit wildlife trafficking, illegal logging, and subsidies that contribute to dangerous overfishing. Rules limiting such activities would help ensure that trade remains sustainable and that its benefits are broadly shared. The TPP countries are also working to ensure fair competition between private firms and state-owned enterprises that receive subsidies or other preferences. And Washington is pushing to protect unrestricted access to the Internet and the free flow of data so that small and medium-sized businesses around the world will be able to access global markets efficiently.

As the need for new rules has grown, so, too, has the difficulty of reaching agreement on the details. Emerging economies such as China and India have pressed for a stronger voice in international matters, but they have been reluctant to take on responsibilities commensurate with their increasing role in the global economy. Earlier this year, for example, a handful of countries led by India blocked the implementation of the WTO's Trade Facilitation Agreement, which seeks to eliminate red tape in border and customs disputes and therefore contribute significantly to economic activity, especially in developing countries. In this and other areas, the United States will continue to press ahead, working with those countries willing to adopt stronger rules and, in doing so, hopefully giving new momentum to the WTO's multilateral efforts.

STRENGTHENING PARTNERS

Trade has played a leading role in many of the most important chapters of U.S. history, often as a tool for strengthening international partnerships and alliances. The best-known example of this occurred in the wake of World War II, when the United States provided more access to Western European countries and Japan than it received from them, in an attempt to speed their reconstruction and solidify their integration into an open, rules-based international order.

Trade also serves as an effective way to send signals to allies and rivals. Signaling was the primary motivation behind the United Kingdom's push for the trade agreement it signed with the United States in 1938, just before the outbreak of World War II. The British gained little economically, but the deal bolstered the appearance of Anglo-American solidarity. Similarly, signaling was as important as economics to the United States' first-ever free-trade agreement, which was concluded with Israel in 1985. If anyone doubts the strategic importance of trade, consider Russia's reaction during the past year to the prospect of Ukraine deepening its trade ties with the West.

The global trading system also provides avenues for peaceful competition and mechanisms for resolving grievances that might otherwise escalate. Over time, the habits of cooperation shaped through trade can reduce misperceptions, build trust, and increase cooperation between states on other issues—creating "an atmosphere congenial to the preservation of peace," as U.S. President Harry Truman put it in 1947, while making the case for the creation of an early international trade organization.

Given recent developments in Asia and Europe—tensions over the East China and South China seas, the crisis in Ukraine—the strategic implications of U.S. trade policy have rarely been clearer. For many of the countries that would be party to the TPP, the economic benefits of the agreement are further sweetened by expectations that the United States will become more deeply embedded in the region. And just as completing the tpp would underscore Washington's commitment to development and stability in Asia during a time of flux, finalizing the Transatlantic Trade and Investment Partnership (T-TIP) would send an unmistakable signal to the world about the strength of the U.S.-European bond—a timely reminder, as the crisis in Ukraine has triggered deep unease across the continent.

The economic ties between the United States and its European trading partners are substantial: $1 trillion in trade each year, $4 trillion in investments, and jobs for 13 million American and European workers whose employment depends on transatlantic trade and investment. T-TIP aims to strengthen those already robust ties by better aligning the regulations and standards that the United States and European countries impose on firms—without compromising the environmental safeguards or health and safety measures that protect consumers on both sides of the Atlantic. From an economic perspective, T-TIP presents an enormous opportunity to increase trade, potentially grow the economies of the United States and its European partners by hundreds of billions of dollars, and support hundreds of thousands of additional jobs. And many in Europe believe that T-TIP will not only spur much-needed economic growth but also support efforts to reform European energy policies and create greater energy security.

KEEP ON GROWING

U.S. trade policy aims not only to update the global economic architecture but also to expand it. In the postwar era, the United States has been a leader in providing market access to developing countries. More people now benefit from the global trading system than at any time in history. Unfortunately, however, what then UN Secretary-General Kofi Annan said at the beginning of this century still remains true: "The main losers in today's very unequal world are not those who are too much exposed to globalization. They are those who have been left out." The world's poorest countries still face significant challenges, but by encouraging good governance and sustainable growth, U.S. trade policy can help alleviate poverty and promote stability.

Trade cannot solve every development challenge, but it is a necessary part of any successful and sustainable development strategy. Trade fuels faster growth, stimulates investment, and promotes competition, which results in more jobs and more income for the poor. Growth and investment, in turn, make it easier for developing countries to finance antipoverty programs and improve public services. This virtuous cycle depends on a number of factors, such as strong institutions, the rule of law, sufficient infrastructure, and quality health care and education. Foreign assistance plays a critical role in many of these areas as well, but over time, truly sustainable growth requires trade and investment.

The link between trade and development has never been stronger than in recent decades. Between 1991 and 2011, developing countries' share of world trade doubled and nearly one billion people escaped poverty. Some of the countries that were most engaged in trade, including many in Asia, saw the greatest progress in development, whereas countries that remained largely closed, including many in the Middle East and North Africa, generally saw substantially less progress. In the mid-1990s, foreign direct investment in developing countries surpassed the amount they received in foreign aid. And last year, for the first time in history, the value of trade between developing countries exceeded that between developing and developed countries.

Trade-led development serves U.S. interests by growing markets for U.S. exports and by preventing conflict. It is also an important expression of American values. U.S. trade policy supports greater competition, more participation in the market, and more rigorous labor and environmental standards. In doing so, U.S. trade policy advances broader definitions of international security, including human security and environmental security.

The United States' commitment to promoting development through trade is at the heart of the African Growth and Opportunity Act, which has opened U.S. markets to a wide array of African exports, including textiles, apparel, horticultural goods, and processed agricultural products. Adopted near the end of the Clinton administration, AGOA has become the cornerstone of U.S. trade policy with sub-Saharan Africa. From 2001 to 2013, U.S. imports covered by AGOA more than tripled, including a nearly fourfold increase in non-oil imports. During the same period, the amount of U.S. direct investment in sub-Saharan countries nearly quadrupled.

AGOA has supported hundreds of thousands of jobs in sub-Saharan Africa, creating economic opportunities that otherwise might not exist. The United States has benefited from the stability that has accompanied this increased prosperity, as well as from the market opportunities AGOA has created for U.S. firms. Since 2001, U.S. exports to the region have more than tripled, and last year, those exports supported nearly 120,000 American jobs. Africa—home to the world's fastest-growing middle classes and several of the world's fastest-growing economies—will likely continue to rise, economically and geopolitically, in the coming years. Still, there is much more to be done. The Obama administration has proposed not just renewing AGOA but also updating it to reflect changes within Africa and between African countries and their trading partners. Doing so would send a strong message to the world that the United States is deeply committed to Africa and to promoting broad-based development through trade.

BUYING IN TO TRADE

The Obama administration's three strategic trade objectives—establishing and enforcing rules of the road, strengthening partnerships, and promoting development—all serve the greater goal of revitalizing the international economic architecture. Establishing and enforcing rules of the road will ensure that tomorrow's global trading system is consistent with American values and interests. Strengthening the United States' partnerships and alliances with other countries will protect that system and lay the foundation for pursuing broader mutual interests. Promoting broad-based, inclusive development will expand that system so that its benefits are both greater and more widely shared.

The economic foundation of the Obama administration's trade agenda is sound, and the strategic stakes of following through with it could not be higher. Given the current constraints on fiscal and monetary policies, there is no better source of growth than trade.

As tensions rise in Asia and on the periphery of Europe, the strategic merits of the TPP and T-TIP become even clearer.

At the same time, Washington faces unprecedented constraints in crafting trade policy. The United States no longer holds as dominant a position in the global economy as it did at the end of World War II, and it must build trade coalitions willing to work toward consensus positions. Meanwhile, the economic struggles facing many Americans have fostered a sense of insecurity and skepticism about the benefits of trade.

Such concerns are legitimate, but too often they reflect a conflation of the impact of technological change and economic globalization with the effects of trade agreements. To help address these worries and better engage Congress, the public, and other stakeholders, the Obama administration has worked to make its trade agenda the most transparent in U.S. history, closely discussing trade issues and negotiations with small-business owners, nongovernmental organizations, and labor unions and holding more than 1,400 congressional briefings on the TPP alone. The Office of the U.S. Trade Representative consults with congressional committees on every proposal the United States makes during trade negotiations, and any member of Congress can review the negotiating texts.

These efforts have given unprecedented weight to public input and congressional oversight. Congress' involvement could be further enhanced and institutionalized by the passage of trade promotion authority, which would allow Congress to guide trade policy by laying out the United States' negotiating objectives, defining how the executive branch must consult with Congress about trade agreements, and detailing the legislative procedures that will guide Congress' consideration of trade agreements. At the same time, by ensuring that Congress will consider trade agreements as they have been negotiated by the executive branch, trade promotion authority would give U.S. trading partners the necessary confidence to put their best and final offers on the table. Trade promotion authority has a long, bipartisan history—stretching back to President

Franklin Roosevelt and the U.S. Congress during the New Deal era—of ensuring congressional oversight while also strengthening the United States' hand at the international bargaining table.

CHOOSE OR LOSE

Trade initiatives such as the TPP, T-TIP, and AGOA give Americans a chance to shape the global economy, rather than just be shaped by it. Increasingly, the rules-based, open trading system is competing with state-directed, mercantilist models. The United States is not alone in working to define the rules of the road in the Asia-Pacific, for example, and not all of the United States' competitors share Washington's commitment to raising labor and environmental standards, enforcing intellectual property rights, ensuring that state-owned enterprises compete fairly with private firms, and maintaining a free and open Internet. Failing to deliver on the Obama administration's agenda would mean missing an opportunity to create safer workplaces, a better environment, and healthier and more open societies. The failure to lead could spill into other domains as others filled the gap.

There is no doubt that it is in the interests of American workers, farmers, and ranchers; manufacturers and service providers; entrepreneurs and inventors for the United States to actively shape the global trading system and promote a race to the top, rather than engage in a race to the bottom. If the United States wants to strengthen its economic power and extend its strategic influence during uncertain times, Washington must make a decision: either lead on global trade or be left on the sidelines. There really is no choice.